How to
Communicate
with
Confidence

How to Communicate with Confidence

MIKE BECHTLE

SPIRE

© 2008 by Mike Bechtle

Published by Revell
a division of Baker Publishing Group
P.O. Box 6287, Grand Rapids, MI 49516-6287
www.revellbooks.com

Previously published under the title *Confident Conversation*
Spire edition published 2013

ISBN 978-0-8007-8834-6

Printed in the United States of America

Published in association with the literary agency of Alive Communications, Inc., 7680 Goddard Street, Suite 200, Colorado Springs, CO 80920.

16   17   18   19   20   21   13   12   11   10   9   8

To Sara
What a privilege that you have honored me
with years of conversation—
the greatest gift a daughter could give a father

Contents

Part Four: Focus Outwardly

Acknowledgments

I used to think that writing a book was hardest on the author. After all, he's the one who spends hours in relative seclusion, picking through words and ideas to form coherent sentences. He's the one who sees the impending deadlines and struggles to get things submitted on time. Lawns get shaggy, cars stay unwaxed, and life priorities get moved to the back burner. In other words, I don't get to do all of the fun stuff until the book is finished.

But this time around, I realized that others pay a greater price than I do. My wife, Diane, watched me disappear both physically and emotionally for a while but remained my greatest champion. No matter how good I get as a writer, I will never be able to choose the right combination of words to fully express my love and gratitude. What an amazing gift she is.

My daughter, Sara, was gracious enough to schedule the birth of her second daughter, Elena, two weeks after my deadline. Times with her and her family are among the things I cherish most. Those have been lacking the past few months, and they are among the first things I plan to reinstate. I treasure my time with them.

My respect and love for my son, Tim, grows exponentially over time. Our schedules and distance always make connecting a challenge, but those times are precious. We've been postponing our trip to Roscoe's Chicken and Waffles until the book was finished. It's done now, so it's time to head to Long Beach for lunch.

Beth Jusino is the kind of agent who can spoil you. Her input, friendship, and guidance have made the past two books a joyous process, and Alive Communications is a better agency because they brought her on board.

Beth's greatest gift to me was offering this book to Vicki Crumpton of Revell. When I found out I would be working with her again, the entire process took on an air of celebration. Seeing her editing skills is like watching Rembrandt paint. She knows how to take my verbal sketches and turn them into a work of art, while still keeping my voice in the writing. It's a privilege to partner with her again.

Everything I've learned about conversation has come because God converses with his people. This book is a grateful expression of his communication in my life.

1

Conversation—One Size *Doesn't* Fit All

Everyone wants to communicate more effectively. That's why you picked up this book. But lasting success won't come from following a set of tips and techniques. Our conversational skills improve when we adapt those techniques to our own unique personality.

I teach seminars for a living. Every day I deal with executives, managers, and line workers in companies ranging from mom-and-pop operations to Fortune 500 companies. I've discovered that no matter what a person's role, education, or income is, they all fit in one of two broad categories:

- Those who have trouble talking
- Those who have trouble listening

In both cases, effective conversation happens when individuals communicate through their own unique strengths and temperament.

When I'm leading a seminar, I've found that about 20 percent of the group members participate aloud. Others will share in a small group but not with the entire class. Still others prefer to sit quietly and take notes.

In school, verbal participation is usually encouraged. In fact, many college courses assign a percentage of the semester grade based on class participation. That's always painful for the quieter class members who learn better by listening but is a reward for those who are naturally more outgoing. I remember forcing myself to ask one question aloud each class period so I could be seen as an active participant. But it didn't make me any smarter. In fact, it hindered my learning because it didn't allow for my unique learning style.

Conversation and Life

Conversation is one of the basic tools for twenty-first-century living. Almost everything we do depends on it. We can't buy a car, negotiate a business deal, or strengthen a relationship without conversation. When it's done effectively, we get satisfying results. When it's done ineffectively, we feel unsatisfied with the outcomes.

But conversation is one thing we don't spend a lot of time trying to improve. We'll pay someone to help us improve our golf swing, learn photography, or develop our computer skills. But when it comes to making conversation, we don't make a conscious effort to develop a skill that can have a huge impact on how well we live each day.

You might feel that when it comes to conversational skills, you're dealt the hand you were given. It's your personality, so you're stuck with it. Maybe you've read a book or article to try to improve but found tips for talking that just seemed too foreign to your temperament. Discouraged, you resigned yourself to making the best of a bad situation.

But the problem isn't having the wrong personality. The problem comes when we try to change who we are to become something we're not. Compensating for perceived weaknesses won't lead to a sense of fulfillment in conversations. Instead, we need to embrace the personality we have and explore ways to capitalize on it. Taking golf lessons doesn't change your body type, but it teaches you to get the most out of the body you have. Why not spend time studying your personality and learning to get the most out of it? The benefits will take you a lot farther than simply improving your putting skills.

Confidence

Jerry Seinfeld quipped that at a funeral most people would rather be in the casket than giving the eulogy. It's also true in more casual settings. Many of us walk into a social gathering assuming that we're the most uncomfortable person in the room. We wonder how people perceive us and try to change our behavior to alter their perception. We feel like we're the lone struggler in a room full of self-confident communicators. In reality, many of the people in the room are thinking the same thing. They're not thriving; they're surviving.

I've often assumed that the confidence I see in everyone else is what they're actually feeling. But I realize that I often try to give off an air of confidence with others even when I'm not feeling that way. If that's what I'm doing, it's realistic to assume that others are doing it too. Imagine what it would be like if everyone said aloud what their emotions were during each conversation:

- "I'm afraid to talk to you, because I'm afraid you won't like me."
- "I'm really intimidated by you."
- "I'm a lot more interested in what I have to say than in what you think."

You Can't Fake Genuine

Most books about conversation focus on tips and techniques to make us appear more confident and interested in others. But it's hard to be something you're not and express feelings you don't have. If you simply try to appear friendlier, you'll have minimal success. Real results come when the change is inside of you.

Publius Syrus, a Roman poet from about 100 BC, said, "We are interested in others when they are interested in us."[1] A more modern communication expert, Dale Carnegie, said, "You can make more friends in two months by becoming genuinely interested in other people than you can in two years by trying to get other people interested in you."[2]

Throughout this book, we'll be focusing on learning to be yourself in conversation. When you're free to express your own personality and relax and enjoy the other person's unique style, real communication can take place.

You Can't Be Something You're Not

Most books on conversation also try to make quieter types into something we're not. I've never considered myself to be shy, but I definitely grew up on the "quiet side." Everyone I knew seemed to be more outgoing than I was, and I envied their ability to strike up a conversation and keep it going. Deep inside, I felt like something was wrong with me.

I had a few friends that I would hang out with who were also introverts, kind of like a "secret society" of quiet people. Occasionally, I would build a relationship with an extrovert and would feel a boost in my self-esteem because a popular person would associate with me. But no matter whom I was talking to, I always wondered how they perceived me. I assumed that they were noticing how uncomfortable I was, as though I were wearing a sign around my neck that said, "Don't ask me about my day."

My solution was to try to *act* like an extrovert. If I could *pretend* to be more outgoing, maybe I could fit in with others. It seemed to help, but it was draining to pretend I was something that I wasn't. I read books and articles about how to be more outgoing and got a lot of good tips. But with my quiet personality, those tips weren't dealing with the real issue. Over time, they made the situation worse; I was an introvert trying to become an extrovert.

And it just didn't happen.

The Desire to Be Different

In moments of honesty, I would admit that I wasn't very happy with my situation. I desperately wanted to be more outgoing. After all, the books about success told me that's what I needed to be effective in life. But the more I tried to change, the less change I saw taking place. I felt like a Volkswagen trying to become a race car.

As a child, I had been taught that God created us as unique individuals with a specific purpose. But as an adult, that perspective presented some uncomfortable implications. If it was true, it meant that I was given a quiet temperament on purpose. That left me with two options:

1. God made a mistake.
2. I have exactly the temperament I need to do what I'm designed to do.

I knew the first option wasn't true. But that left me with a dilemma: If my personality wasn't a mistake, then it also wasn't something to be "fixed." It might actually be a *good* thing. So either I could continue feeling shortchanged, or I would have to learn how to accept my personality and even celebrate it!

I discovered that I wasn't alone. Even my extrovert contacts seemed to struggle at times with making effective conversation. They might be more outgoing and comfortable in a conversation, but they didn't obtain the outcomes they were expecting. They felt like they were communicating clearly, but the other person didn't respond well. These extroverts didn't have trouble *talking*; they needed help understanding their listeners and seeing through their eyes.

That's where my journey began. Over time, I began to understand the value of uniqueness. Whether we're on the quiet side or the expressive side, we're not a mistake. The more we try to change our personality into something we're not, the more frustrated we'll become. We don't need to change our personality; we need to understand it, embrace it, develop it, learn from it, and capitalize on it.

Starting the Journey

The secret to confident conversation is to develop skills that fit our personality style, discover the personality style of the person we're talking to, and find a way to make those styles work together. We don't have to become like the other person; we have to become like "ourselves."

My wife and I moved into a new house a couple of weeks ago. We left a house we lived in for sixteen years that reflected our personality and tastes. The new house hasn't been updated in thirty years. Walking through it today, we felt overwhelmed with the task ahead. We love the floor plan, but it feels like it will take years to look like "us." It's discouraging and seems like a monumental task.

How will we do it? One task at a time. We'd like it to be perfect overnight, but we know that's not realistic. Our satisfaction will come in appreciating the little changes that will take place, rather than feeling the frustration of how much needs to be done.

Developing confidence in your conversational ability is the same way. For people who feel ineffective at interaction, it seems like a monumental task. After all, we've been using our current techniques for a lifetime. Change will occur in bite-sized pieces as we experiment with new perceptions and processes. When we focus on little changes in our skill set, we'll find encouragement. If we focus on how much more growth needs to occur, we'll only find frustration.

For some people, learning to communicate effectively requires a total remodeling job, while others simply need a fresh coat of paint. Conversational skill levels vary, but everyone could use a little "spring cleaning" now and then. This book will be a resource to strengthen anyone's skills, whether it involves gaining new skills or just sharpening the ones they have.

I have to open cardboard boxes almost daily, unpacking materials for seminars I teach. For years I used my car keys to cut through the tape. One day I purchased a tiny box cutter. Now I wonder how I ever survived without it. When we use tools for the purpose for which they were designed, we find a new level of freedom.

Your uniqueness will determine what you take from this book.

If you're an extrovert, you'll learn about communication styles that differ from yours and how to best work with them. You'll discover your own uniqueness and develop a plan for capitalizing on that uniqueness. Everyday encounters can be strengthened as you become sensitive to the needs of the other person.

If you're an introvert, this will be a "preparedness kit." In California, many people have "earthquake preparedness kits" to help them survive a natural disaster. It contains the basic tools and supplies to make it through the first few days of a crisis—water, batteries, lights, food, and so on. You may not need all the tools all the time, but you'll have them ready when you need them.

In this book, we'll provide plenty of "supplies" for the journey. You'll learn:

- How to customize conversational techniques to fit that temperament
- How to start, continue, and end a conversation
- How to handle tough conversations
- How to use electronic communication effectively
- How to listen deeply to others
- How to ask questions effectively
- How to be *yourself*

Decide what you'd like to get out of this book. Start by writing down what you want to accomplish by improving your conversational skills. Do you want to be able to approach people more easily, or hold your own in a conversation with your bosses, or be able to mingle well at a social event? Get a clear picture of what you would like to accomplish.

Hope for the Journey

We're surrounded by advertising that tells us we're not good enough the way we are. Commercials and print ads are based on making us feel dissatisfied and inadequate: If we only had whiter teeth, more money, less weight, and better technology, our problems would be over. The ads are saying, "People will like you if you could just be different than you are."

But trying to be something we're not only leads to frustration when we try these "one-size-fits-all" methods. Hope for genuine success comes from being genuine.

If we want to see short-term change, we can try different behaviors. But if we want exponential change, we need to change the way we think—our attitudes and perceptions about the process. It involves gaining an understanding that we're not flawed; we just have a different set of tools than other people do. We rob ourselves and others when we ignore the tools and skills we have, trying to become like someone else.

In this book, we'll learn to discover the tools we have and the unique advantages we have over other people. This isn't a book about personality types, but we'll look at them to gain a basic understanding of why people are different and why that's good. We'll look at our uniqueness to explore the other person's uniqueness. When that happens, we'll move our conversations to a whole different level.

As you begin your journey, just remember:

You don't have to be different.

You don't have to be better.

You have to be *you*!

○○○○○○○○○○

PART ONE

Function Uniquely

2

Unique by Design

I'm not sure how old I was, but I saw a cartoon in which someone had a magic wand. She would touch something with it, and the object would magically change into whatever she desired. So I cut a branch off my parents' apricot tree and hoped for the best.

I wished for a lot of things that day. Toys, wealth, and popularity were probably high on the list. But among other wishes, I do remember tapping myself on the head with that branch and saying, "I wish I weren't so quiet."

I wasn't exactly shy, but I felt that everyone around me had a much easier time in making conversation than I did. I would analyze the conversations my friends would have during recess, thinking, *Why is it so easy for them?* When I would participate, I was always worried about how I was coming across to them. My biggest fear was saying something stupid and having them laugh at me.

By the time I reached high school I had picked up a few

social survival skills but still found the process unnatural. One day in my freshman year, I ended up standing behind Jack in the cafeteria line. He was a popular senior—the quarterback of the football team. I knew him by reputation but certainly would never try to have a conversation with him. But he turned around and said, "Hey—how are you?" I remember being so stunned that I couldn't even answer him. After a few uncomfortable seconds he said, "So are you shy, or what?" I think I managed to form a few words in response but beat myself up for days at my failure to communicate.

I didn't like the way I was. I thought it was unfair. I thought I was the only one who felt that way. I wanted to change. I wanted to be an extrovert. I wanted a magic wand that worked.

Years later, I finally found it. But it looked a lot different than I expected.

The Magic of Uniqueness

When we're in a group of people, many of us tend to gravitate toward those who are most like us. We're more comfortable with those people because we can find common ground more quickly. When we're around people who are completely different from us, it takes a lot more work to find points of similarity. Or so we may think.

Life would be so boring if we were all alike. Think about the advantages of each of us being unique:

1. Life is more exciting that way.
2. We value the uniqueness in others.
3. Making conversation is actually easier.

1. *Life is more exciting that way.*

My grandfather loved orange marmalade. Whether he had toast, muffins, or pancakes, he always used it. Day after day, it was orange marmalade.

My dad, on the other hand, kept a variety of jams and jellies in the cupboard. He might choose strawberry jam one day for his toast, cherry the next day, and grape the next. But I noticed there was no orange marmalade in his collection. When I asked him why, he simply said, "It's boring."

Differences add richness to life. Looking back over my life, there have been times when everything went smoothly and I was comfortable. I liked those times and would love to have more of them. But the most satisfying memories I have are the unique, challenging situations that I survived. They weren't necessarily pleasant at the time, but they make up the most interesting parts of my personal history.

Many of us have driven through long, sunny stretches of desert and fought our way through powerful rainstorms on winding mountain roads. Most of us would choose the straight highways whenever possible—but we know what it's like to fight drowsiness on those trips. On the stormy trips, drowsiness isn't usually an issue. Our senses are heightened, and we're desperately aware of the need to stay focused. When we reach our destination, which story do we repeat weeks later—the quiet, straight-highway stories or the life-threatening adventure in the stormy hills?

I believe God created each of us to be unique. Our personalities are different by design. The richness in our lives comes from those differences.

2. *We value the uniqueness in others.*

Sometimes it's easy to take our uniqueness for granted. It's not just snowflakes and fingerprints that are unique; each of us has a unique blend of physical characteristics and personality styles. We weren't created from a template or an assembly line. We're a unique combination of physical, emotional, mental, and spiritual characteristics that is different from every other person. We're a one-of-a-kind work of art, which means we each have a unique purpose to offer that no one else has.

The psalmist said, "You created my inmost being; you knit me together in my mother's womb" (Ps. 139:13). I believe God custom-designed each of us with a unique blend of physical characteristics and personality styles. Design implies function, which means that the uniqueness of our design implies the uniqueness of our function. Nobody else is like you, so you'll be most effective when you function out of your unique design.

3. *Making conversation is actually easier.*

Most people enter a conversation searching for common ground with another person. It sounds logical that the more similarities there are between you and that person, the easier the conversation would be, right?

It may be true that those conversations are easier to start. But they run out of steam pretty quickly. If we were all the same, conversation would be like talking to ourselves. The more differences there are between people, the more ingredients can be added to the conversation. Those differences provide new topics to explore, which makes it easier to take the conversation in new directions.

Different Strokes

We commonly call people who have difficulty talking "introverts." And we might call people who talk a mile a minute but have trouble stopping to listen "extroverts." But that's not the whole story.

First, let's define our terms. *Introverts* are people who gain energy when they have time alone. They aren't necessarily shy, but they need their "space" to regroup after being in a group setting. They tend to process internally, rather than thinking aloud with others. They might not participate easily in a group discussion but think through the issues later on their own. Often their conclusions are solid and well thought out, even though it might take them longer to arrive at those conclusions. They tend to think *before* speaking.

Those with "talking" problems struggle with issues such as:

- How they come across to others
- Saying the right thing
- Getting tongue-tied
- Initiating a conversation

Extroverts gain energy when they're surrounded by others. The bigger the group, the more energized they become. They often do their best thinking aloud and shape their opinions while talking with others. They're quick on their feet and aren't intimidated by speaking up in a group setting. Their initial conclusions might not be as deep, but they realize that it's part of the process to get to the final conclusions. They tend to think *by* speaking.

Those with "listening" problems have to deal with:

- Why people don't always agree with them
- Getting bored in a conversation
- Why some people seem uncomfortable around them
- Understanding what quiet people bring to a conversation

Is one style better?

Introverts often wish they could be more like extroverts, free to engage in conversations quickly and easily. But they're focusing on only one aspect of temperament. In the same way, extroverts might wonder why their co-workers' eyes glaze over when they start talking.

Both temperaments bring critical uniqueness to any relationship. Introverts add depth to a discussion, while extroverts make sure action takes place. Eliminate the introverts, and you could end up with half-baked decisions that fail when implemented. Get rid of the extroverts, and you might have carefully designed plans that never leave the drawing board.

The more we try to be something we're not designed to be, the more frustrated we'll become. Our personality type isn't "the problem"—it can become the source of our ability to work with others. The more we try to become like someone else, the more we rob ourselves and others of the uniqueness we bring to the table. If we're uncomfortable about our temperament, it's because we're comparing ourselves with others instead of capitalizing on our own strengths.

There are two foundational realities that make conversation effective:

- Understanding and accepting who you really are
- Understanding and accepting who the other person is

That perspective will eliminate a large percentage of the conversational issues we face, because we're communicating with integrity instead of playing games to impress each other.

A Step at a Time or the Quick Fix

John wants to own a home. He barely makes it from paycheck to paycheck and always runs out of money before he runs out of month. He wishes things were different but feels trapped. Each week he buys five lottery tickets, hoping that his dream will come true. Statistically, his chances of winning are almost nonexistent. Nevertheless, he's betting on a quick fix to all his troubles.

I asked my accountant friend Steve to run the numbers for me. What if John didn't buy lottery tickets and invested the money instead? What would the results be if he invested $5 each week at, say, 5 percent interest? After forty years, that weekly $5 would be worth over $33,000. That means he could make more by *not* playing the lottery than most people do actually playing it, and it's an outcome that's not left to chance.

How does that apply to our conversational skills?

We can't change our basic temperament; it's out of our control. Trying to remake our personality style seems to offer a quick fix, but it only leads to frustration. I believe there's a better way.

The key is to take a closer look at our uniqueness, accept it, and embrace it.

Once we recognize the *value* of our own unique strengths and characteristics, we can use that as a starting place to build our conversational skills. It becomes the foundation on which to add new skills and techniques. We'll begin to interact honestly with others instead of trying to "come across" in a certain way that's artificial.

There isn't a quick fix to make us great conversationalists overnight. But this book gives you a blueprint for making it happen one step at a time. It's a lifelong growth process based on the beauty of our uniqueness.

Making Magic

Your uniqueness and the uniqueness of those around you opens the door to confident conversation. *Celebrating our uniqueness* is the greatest tool we have for building relationships and making conversation. When we focus on who we are and quit trying to be somebody else, that's when the magic happens.

3

What's Your Style?

My son-in-law, Brian, loves to be in the center of big events. He's most comfortable in a stadium full of people, a room that's buzzing with conversation, or a crowded party. His only regret is that when the group is too large, he can't meet everyone. When the Star Wars sequels premiered, he spent the day in Hollywood just to experience the energy. Opening day at any theater is his first choice for a movie, because every seat will be filled. He feeds on the noise and the excitement.

I, on the other hand, wait for the last day a film is playing. That way I can enjoy the movie in a mostly empty room. A few times, I've had the luxury of being the only person in the theater. When that happens, I feel as if I've been given a gift—a couple of hours of solitude. If someone walks in late, I feel like they've stolen something from me.

Brian and I don't go to movies together very often . . .

It's hard for me to understand how someone can enjoy a crowd for very long. And I'm sure Brian wonders how anyone can tolerate the silence. People with such strong feelings tend to take one of two perspectives:

1. "Something's wrong with me."
2. "Something's wrong with you."

The first perspective is typical of an introvert. The second perspective is often characteristic of an extrovert.

We live in an extrovert society. Not totally, but since extroverts talk more, they're the ones we hear from the most. We're surrounded by messages that imply the need to communicate more forcefully, directly, and effectively.

Go to any bookstore and you'll find shelves of self-help books written to help people become more outgoing. Who writes those books? Extroverts. Who can best use the tools they offer? Extroverts. Who usually buys those books? Introverts.

Many of these books suggest techniques for being an effective conversationalist. They imply that the more techniques you use, the better you'll perform. But if those techniques don't mesh with your personality and temperament, they'll simply be a source of frustration. When they don't work, introverts assume that *they're* the problem, not the techniques—and they feel like a failure. So the place to begin isn't practicing dozens of different techniques. It's taking the time to discover your own temperament and personality style. Then you can pick the techniques that mesh with who you really are, providing a solid base for effective communication.

Finding the Real "You"

Researchers turn out a seemingly endless stream of information about personality differences, and their results touch almost every area of our lives:

- Businesses use personality inventories to screen job applicants and place them in appropriate work positions.
- Counselors use them to help patients understand relational and emotional issues.
- Individuals take them to find out why they handle life the way they do.

One of the most common instruments, the Myers-Briggs Type Inventory, has been around since the early 1900s—and is still in use. The results help categorize people in a grid of four different continuums:

- Extroversion vs. Introversion (drawing one's energy from other people vs. recharging when alone)
- Sensing vs. Intuiting (evaluating the world through the senses vs. seeing patterns and possibilities in that world)
- Thinking vs. Feeling (making logic-based decisions vs. using intuition to decide)
- Perceiving vs. Judging (recognizing a type of flower vs. deciding it would look good displayed in one's house)[3]

Roger Von Oech suggests four categories of personality:

- Explorers (those who love discovering brand-new ideas)
- Artists (those who shape those ideas into workable proposals)

- Judges (those who analyze those ideas to see if they will work)
- Warriors (those who focus on getting those ideas put into action)

He suggests that explorers and artists tend to be right-brained, creative types of people, while judges and warriors are left-brained and analytical. All of them are important:

- Without Explorers you'll never have any new ideas.
- Without Artists you won't have enough structure to your ideas to make them work.
- Without Judges you'll implement ideas that will fail for lack of scrutiny.
- Without Warriors you'll have great ideas, but nothing will get done.[4]

John Trent took a user-friendly approach to personalities, suggesting four categories from the animal world:

- *Lions* are natural leaders who take charge and make decisions easily. They're goal oriented, but their directness doesn't give much grace to others.
- *Beavers* are organized and take the time to do everything right. They play by the rules and can be perfectionists, having unrealistic expectations of others to do the same.
- *Otters* are outgoing and talkative, connecting well with other people. They have lots of friends, but fewer deep relationships. While pursuing social situations, they tend to lack discipline and follow-through.

- *Golden Retrievers* have a calming effect on relationships. They're loyal to a few close friends and are comfortable to be around. They thrive on encouragement but tend to be indecisive.[5]

These are just a few of the myriad approaches to discovering personality. They each have their place, and spending time studying them can give valuable insight to various parts of our personalities.

Since we're talking about the process of making conversation, we'll keep it simple by looking at just two major categories:

- *Introverts* (people who are energized when alone)
- *Extroverts* (people who are energized by being around others)

The other perspectives could add value, but these two categories will provide a simple framework that most people can identify with. With a clear understanding of those categories, it will be easier to do further reading to incorporate the other approaches.

In or Out?

Some people are firmly on the extrovert scale, while others clearly find themselves on the introvert side. But most people find themselves somewhere in between, a combination of characteristics of both temperaments. Let's see where you find yourself on the continuum.

For each of the following questions, circle the letter corresponding to the answer that best applies to you. You might feel that none of the answers directly apply, or that more than one is true. For those questions, simply select the one that comes closest to describing your situation.

1. People often describe me as
   a. analytical.
   b. disciplined.
   c. creative.
2. After I've had several days filled with social interaction (such as attending a multiday conference)
   a. I resume my regular activities with renewed energy.
   b. I resume my regular activities with normal energy.
   c. I tend to "crash" and have trouble focusing for the next day or so.
3. I enjoy having people stay at my house
   a. for an indefinite period of time.
   b. for a week.
   c. for a couple of days.
4. When something needs to be done, I tend to
   a. jump in and take action.
   b. read the instructions before taking action.
   c. procrastinate.
5. After spending a lot of time in a group or social setting
   a. I have more energy than before the event.
   b. I have about the same amount of energy.
   c. I feel drained of energy.
6. When I'm talking with someone
   a. I'm more aware of what they are saying than what they might be feeling.

b. I can sense there is more under the surface than they're saying, but I focus more on the conversation.

c. Somehow, I can just sense what a person is feeling or thinking (beyond their words).

7. When I buy something that doesn't fit

a. I take it back to the store immediately.

b. I don't really like taking it back, but I return it when I get a chance.

c. I keep it.

8. When I have a free evening

a. I'll call some friends so we can go out together.

b. I'll invite a few close friends over to my place.

c. I'll spend the evening alone with a good book or video.

9. When I attend a comfortable social event

a. I wish the event would keep going, and I'm usually the last one to leave.

b. I enjoy the event and leave when everyone else does.

c. I look forward to the end, even if I enjoy the event.

10. When it comes to friends

a. I want as many as possible.

b. I like having a lot of casual friends and a few close ones.

c. I prefer to have a few deep relationships.

11. When people describe my conversational skills

a. they say I have a "gift of gab."

b. they say I'm comfortable to be with.

c. they say I'm a good listener.

12. When someone asks for my opinion, I'll usually say,

    a. "Great. Here's exactly what I think about it."

    b. "Interesting. Tell me more . . ."

    c. "Great question. Let me think about it for a few days and I'll email you my thoughts."

13. My favorite way to communicate is

    a. by phone.

    b. in person.

    c. by email.

14. When I work on a detailed task or assignment

    a. I jump in and work through it from start to finish.

    b. I work in focused "spurts," then take a break to regroup and plan my next move.

    c. I break it down into bite-sized pieces to keep from getting overwhelmed.

15. When I'm a participant in a meeting

    a. I share my ideas openly.

    b. I think a lot and share my ideas occasionally.

    c. I listen carefully without sharing and then develop my ideas later when I'm alone.

16. If I see someone sitting alone in a restaurant

    a. I feel sorry for them and want to join them to keep them company.

    b. I wonder why they're alone but don't feel the desire to find the reason.

    c. I assume they're enjoying their time away from interaction with others.

17. If I'm attending a crowded, noisy meeting or event
    a. I'm energized by the group and try to meet as many people as possible.
    b. I'll talk to someone for a while and then do the same with two or three others.
    c. I'll have an extended conversation with one or two "safe" people; once or twice I'll step outside to get a little "space."

18. If I go out to dinner with friends
    a. I prefer going with a big group to a noisy, energy-filled restaurant where you have to shout to be heard.
    b. I prefer going with a few friends to a family-style restaurant where it's busy but not quite as difficult to converse.
    c. I prefer going with one or two friends to a quiet restaurant where it's easy to make conversation.

19. When I'm in my car trying to find an address
    a. I can easily look for the location while thinking about other things.
    b. I talk out loud as I'm figuring out the directions.
    c. I turn down the radio so I can think clearly without distractions.

20. When I find myself in an airplane or train row with no other passengers, I feel
    a. disappointed.
    b. neutral.
    c. relieved.

Give yourself three points for each "A" answer, two points for each "B," and one point for each "C." Here's what your score says about you:

46–60—You're most likely an extrovert. Like a solar panel, you get your energy from being around others and thrive in group situations. You're not afraid to share your ideas with others, and you think quickly on your feet. That means you're comfortable in conversations, and you shape your ideas by talking about them. The more friends you have, the better. Talking is more natural for you than writing; if someone sends you an email, you might pick up the phone and call them instead of replying in writing. In general, your mind allows you to do several things at once.

31–45—Depending on the situation, you exhibit characteristics of both extroverts and introverts. Social situations are enjoyable but draining if you spend too long at the event. You have a strong need to spend time alone recharging. But once you've gained back your energy, you'll be restless if you don't find people to interact with. The cycle continues if the event lasts longer than you expected, and you find the need to pull away again. It's easy to think through issues during a conversation, but you always clarify your thoughts later when you've had a chance to think alone. You need to spend time in both worlds (extrovert and introvert) to recover from the effects of each.

20–30—You're most likely an introvert. Even though you might not be shy, you find group situations draining the longer they last. You need time alone to restore your energy, much like a rechargeable battery. You enjoy conversations with two or three good friends more than a lot of casual acquaintances. In most conversations, you think of the perfect thing to say about thirty minutes after the conversation is over. That's because you tend to shape your ideas when you're alone in a quiet environment. You're a good listener because you tend to think deeply and focus on one issue at a time. When someone leaves you a voice mail, you prefer to reply in writing so you can craft your response to express exactly what you're thinking.

Greener Grass

My neighbor's lawn always looked better than mine. All I saw in my own lawn were the dead spots, the weeds, and the crabgrass. Since his always looked perfect, I wondered what he did differently. I figured his soil was better or he used a better fertilizer or something. In fact, looking down my street, it seemed that my lawn was the worst on the block.

But one day I stood on my neighbor's lawn and discovered what I hadn't noticed before. He had the same dead spots, weeds, and crabgrass that I had. Looking back at my own yard, it looked perfect. From the top looking down, I could see all the things that were wrong. From a distance where the defects were hidden, I could see all the things that were right.

It's a matter of perspective.

The same thing is true of personalities. When we live in our own skin, we look down and see all the defects—the things we'd like to change. We see other people conversing in a different way, and they appear to be completely comfortable. It's easy to wish we were more like them. We see the good parts of their personality and the bare spots, weeds, and crabgrass of our own. But they're thinking the same thing.

Wishing for a different lawn doesn't make my grass greener. The solution is to analyze what kind of grass I have, test the soil to analyze the ground conditions, and learn the best ways to care for the lawn I have. That way I can plant the right kind of seed to fill in the bare spots, fertilize properly, and apply the right soil conditioner and water. If I plant someone else's type of grass in my bare spots, the lawn will always look splotchy and uneven.

The same is true for our conversational skills. The key isn't trying to imitate someone else; it's becoming a student of ourselves. Once we accept our unique design, we can learn how to capitalize on that uniqueness. We can choose the right conversational techniques, practice in a safe environment, and relate to others in an effective, comfortable way.

So how do we grow our effectiveness at making conversation? By taking care of our own lawn instead of looking at the neighbor's. The grass might appear greener across the fence. But it *becomes* greener in our own yard when we take the time to nurture what we already have.

PART TWO

Prepare Thoroughly

4

Overcoming Barriers

Making conversation sounds like a pretty straightforward process: one person talks, the other person listens. They reverse the process several times until the conversation is finished. Each person understands exactly what the other person was saying, and each person feels totally understood. Right?

Let's say that I have an idea in my head that I want to express to you. My goal is for you to know exactly what I'm thinking. Wouldn't it be nice if we could transfer the information digitally so it would arrive in your head in exactly the same form it was in my head?

Since that's not an option, I have to use another method: words. They can be spoken or written, but that's the medium humans use to connect with each other. So I select the words that best express what I'm thinking, and you receive those words. Sound good so far?

The problem is the meaning we both give to the same words. The words I choose come through a series of filters, such as:

- Language
- Background
- Education
- Socioeconomic status
- Culture

So what seem like neutral words are actually packed with meaning for me. But when you hear those words, you have your own series of filters to interpret them. I might mean one thing, but you hear the same words and get a totally different idea.

For example, I might say "It's hot today." I grew up in the Phoenix desert, so "hot" means something totally different to me than a person from Alaska. Residents of Georgia have still another filter (a humid one) to interpret their concept of heat.

With all those filters, it's amazing that we actually manage to communicate at all! Looking at the same words through different filters creates barriers to effective conversation. Knowing that those filters exist can go a long way toward building mutual understanding.

How Filters Become Barriers

Is there a food that you don't like—that you've never tasted? Even though you haven't tried it, you're convinced that it doesn't taste good. Maybe it's a certain kind of vegetable or an exotic meat. You just know intuitively that you won't like it, and you have no intention of testing your theory.

For me, it's sushi. I haven't tried it, but I'm convinced that it's not good. I grew up around sushi in Arizona, but we called it "bait." I don't eat bait.

The things we believe determine what we do. If we believe a certain food isn't good, we don't eat it. That belief might be right or wrong, but it can become a filter that determines our actions. Those actions produce results. When we don't like the results we're getting, it means that our filters have produced barriers to getting the results we want.

Linda becomes the new manager of a department and is told by the exiting manager that all the people on the team are incompetent. When Linda steps into the new job, she sees her people through that filter, assuming that they're incompetent. So, what does she do? She starts micromanaging them. What kind of results do you get when people are micromanaged? Disloyalty, frustration, and poor performance.

Linda sees the poor performance and assumes the filter is correct: her people are incompetent. So she micromanages even more, causing a downward spiral of resentment. Her filter has become a barrier to managing her people effectively.

Instead of increasing her micromanagement, what if Linda challenged her filter? She could say, "These people might have been incompetent in the past, but they might become more competent if someone believed in them and encouraged them." With that new filter, she has removed the barrier. Her actions would reflect that belief, and she would affirm their skills and strengths. The results of that encouragement could be a stronger team with continually improving performance.

Our success in making conversation depends on whether or not the filters we have create barriers.

A New Way of Thinking

Jeremy works for a major national bank. During his training, he was taught the subtleties of conversation with customers. For example, he was taught how to read a person's handshake. If you shake hands and the other person's hand is on top of yours, it shows that they want to have some control of the conversation. If your hand ends up on top, it means they are expecting you to take the initiative. Then he was taught conversational choices to make based on what he observed.

Jeremy expressed his frustration with the process, which focused more on manipulating clients than genuinely caring about them. When we have similar experiences, we become suspicious of all such techniques. Those experiences become barriers to effective conversation.

If your experience with books or seminars on conversation has been awkward or ineffective in the past, you might not be very excited about more tips and techniques. You feel the need strongly enough to read this book, but you're worried that you'll have to stretch too far outside your comfort zone to make it a reality. Or, you're thinking that the techniques will make it possible, but they will always be uncomfortable.

The bad news is that you're right—about the tips and techniques. If you simply pick random ideas that are foreign to you and force them into your conversations, the process will continue to be painful. The good news is that when you select only the techniques and tips that match your temperament and personality, you've removed that barrier, and you will find conversing with others to be exciting, fulfilling, and fun. That's the goal—to provide customized tools to help you actually enjoy the process of communication. After all—if the process and the result aren't enjoyable, you'll probably give up.

Negative experiences leave us with three options for improving our communication:

1. Avoid making conversation with people.
2. Make conversation but do it poorly and painfully.
3. Analyze our unique personality and learn skills to connect with others.

You may have lived with the first two for a long time. Now it's time to use the third one to remove barriers and gain new skills for effective communication.

Breaking the Sound Barriers

When we don't have complete information about another person's perspective, we tend to make assumptions about what they're thinking. Unfortunately, once we've made those assumptions, we've also decided that they're true. Then we act on the basis of what we believe is true, even if it isn't.

We tell ourselves things such as:

- "They're confident in this conversation, and I'm not."
- "If this conversation is going to work, I have to make them like me."
- "I have to be in control of where this conversation goes."
- "I'm too quiet to make this conversation work."
- "I have to be prepared with lots of conversational topics."

When these barriers characterize our self-talk, we set ourselves up for failure. We believe what we're telling ourselves and then act based on those assumptions. The key is to recognize what we're telling ourselves and then rewrite each assumption into one that's more accurate.

Let's look at some possible "rewrites" of the above barriers:

Old: "They're confident in this conversation, and I'm not."

New: *"I really don't know what they're thinking; they might not be as comfortable as they appear on the surface."*

Any time two people are in conversation, it takes effort to make it effective. It's human nature to want to appear confident, so most people work to seem calmer than they actually feel. The old example of a duck applies here: he seems to be floating smoothly on the surface of the water, but underneath he's paddling like crazy.

If we always feel that we're the only one who's uncomfortable in a conversation, it puts the pressure on us to perform. We feel that it's up to us whether or not the conversation is successful. But much like a successful marriage, it takes both parties to make it work.

Old: "If this conversation is going to work, I have to make them like me."

New: *"I'm not responsible for how the other person feels about me; I just have to be myself."*

When my wife and I went through premarital counseling, we were reminded that it's never accurate to say, "You make me so angry." Anger is a choice that we make. I can say or do something that my wife could respond to in anger—but she could also choose a different response. I'm only responsible for my choices, not another person's reactions.

In conversation, the only effective place to focus our efforts is on being ourselves. I can't make another person like me. But if I can be genuine, it gives the other person a chance to respond to the "real me." If that person doesn't respond the way I'd like her to, it doesn't mean I'm a bad person. It simply means that she is choosing to respond that way, and it's out of my control. The more I try to control the other person, the more frustrated I'll become.

Old: "I have to be in control of where this conversation goes."

New: *"Both of us are responsible for where this conversation goes."*

There are no guarantees that every conversation will be effective and comfortable. But when a conversation doesn't go well, we can't assume responsibility for failure. Just as it takes two or more people to hold a conversation, it takes those same people to determine the outcome.

It's like playing checkers. We might have different skill levels at playing, but neither player is totally responsible for the outcome. No one knows what moves he is going to make at the beginning of the game, since those decisions will be based on what the other player does. It's a dynamic process, with both players using the best of their skills to make an enjoyable game.

There is a difference, however, between checkers and conversation. In checkers, there will be a winner and a loser. In conversation, the goal is for both people to win.

Old: "I'm too quiet to make this conversation work."

New: *"I can learn skills to converse effectively based on my own personality."*

Most introverts feel that they just don't have the tools necessary to be effective in making conversation. Usually, it's because they've been told that the tools they need are "extrovert" tools. But the unique tools of an introvert aren't inferior to those of an extrovert. They bring richness to a conversation that can't be found in any other way. Once introverts gain a clear understanding of what they have to offer, it frees them from the need to "compete" with an extrovert's skill set. They can learn to celebrate those unique abilities because they become the foundation for making stimulating, engaging conversation with others.

Old: "I have to be prepared with lots of conversational topics."

New: *"I need to be a good listener to pick up on things to talk about."*

One of the biggest fears people have is running out of things to say. We might get a conversation started and maintain it for a while, but we dread the silence that comes when we've used up our supply of fresh material.

That approach says that conversational success depends solely on what we bring to a conversation. We assume that if we have a good supply of topics, questions, and stories, we'll be able to drop them in as needed. But that ignores one of the greatest resources for learning to converse effectively: the ability to explore another person's experience for new areas of conversation. We'll examine this point in more detail in the next chapter.

We need to change our role from "Supplier" to "Explorer." That's the most effective way to turn our hesitation into dynamic, fulfilling interactions.

Learning to Explore

An explorer goes into the wilderness without knowing what he'll find. He would probably be more comfortable if he brought supplies for every possible situation, but he would be too loaded down to make the trip. So he brings the tools essential for survival: a compass, water, maps, matches, and other resources to handle the situations he might encounter. He makes sure he knows well how to use the tools before beginning the trip.

It's overwhelming to enter a conversation thinking we need to know everything about everything, just in case it comes up. But if we can discern what tools are essential for communication, we can gain confidence to embark on the adventure. We don't need every tool there is; we just need to become proficient with the best tools—the ones that "fit" our personality.

We don't become seasoned explorers overnight. We can start slowly, using our new tools to venture into new areas. Over time, we gain confidence, which allows us to grow into deeper levels of comfort in conversations.

When our kids were little, they learned to ride bikes. At first, they had training wheels. They were scared but became quite proficient at making circles around the driveway. Gradually, they developed a sense of balance and the training wheels came off. But that didn't mean we sent them on errands five miles away. They stayed in the driveway as their confidence grew. Their range expanded to the sidewalk between our house and the neighbor's driveway. They learned to watch for cars and how to spot other hazards. It was a big day when we finally allowed them to go completely around the block by themselves.

They don't ride their bikes much anymore. But those basic skills turned into the ability to drive a car. They've become comfortable with the skills of finding their way around a city, and they experience the freedom that comes from knowing how to use those skills.

In the rest of this book, we'll be focusing on how to become a skilled Explorer. For an introvert, taking on that role will be the key to gaining the confidence needed to excel in making conversation. For an extrovert, it will provide the tools to make conversations more effective than they've ever been in the past.

Making conversation is like two porcupines that fall in love. They want to be close, but they keep sticking each other. However, since they want to stay warm, they work on making those subtle adjustments that will allow them to stay connected.

In conversation, we try to connect with another person. They might not be just like us, and maybe our encounter is uncomfortable at first. But we have the need for human connection, so we persist—not in becoming like the other person but in acquiring and developing the tools we need to make the conversation work.

5

Common Ground

The phone call came on Monday: "Can you fly to Mexico City tomorrow to teach a seminar on Wednesday?"

Normally, my first thoughts are about logistics: arranging flights and hotels, finding the seminar location, and making the appropriate contacts. But this time, my first question was, "Do they speak English?" My Spanish consisted of the one phrase my grandmother knew: *Cómo se llama su gato?* (What's your cat's name?) It could be a handy question in the right circumstances, but I wasn't sure I could turn it into a full-day seminar.

I was assured that I would be working with people from a number of Latin American countries who spoke at least broken English. With that reassurance, I made the trip.

The company sent a driver to pick me up at the airport for the three-hour drive to the hotel. I assumed that he would be able to communicate in English, but that wasn't the case. Somehow he figured out who I was and approached me as I came into the terminal. When he showed me a paper with my name and flight information on it, I assured him that he had the right person. I followed him to the parking garage.

The language barrier was immediately obvious. I made a few simple comments in English about the crowded terminal, the weather, and the time of day. He just smiled and raised his hands to acknowledge his lack of understanding. He also made a few comments; I smiled and raised my hands in the same way. It was obvious that our long ride would be a quiet one.

When he didn't understand me, I found myself speaking a bit louder or more slowly, assuming that would make a difference. But there was no getting around one simple fact: he didn't speak my language, and I didn't speak his. Nothing I could do would change that.

Mostly, we just smiled at each other. We couldn't understand each other's words, but we could smile. Somehow, that began to cause a connection between us. As he drove, we accepted the language barrier and looked for other ways to communicate. The best moment came when he remembered something he had in his glove compartment. He reached over, fumbled through a careless pile of cassette tapes, and pulled one out. His huge smile appeared as he showed me one he had obviously made himself, with the words "American Music" handwritten on the label with a blue marker. We both laughed as he proudly inserted the tape and turned up the volume. Who would have thought that old Sonny and Cher songs could be the common ground between two people?

As we drove through a particularly low-income area, he pointed to the poverty around us. He frowned, touched his eyes, and traced the path that tears would take, indicating his sadness over the conditions around us. We passed a military compound where he formed his hand into a gun to indicate what we were seeing. He signaled a proud "thumbs-up" as we passed several high-rise buildings that were obviously a source of pride for the city.

Bridging the Gap

To communicate effectively with my driver, I had three choices:

1. I could learn Spanish.
2. He could learn English.
3. We could find some other common ground.

The first option would work in future conversations but wouldn't help me at that moment. Plus, those language skills would be useless if my next driver spoke French or Portuguese. The second option is also unrealistic and presumes that it's the other person's responsibility to make the communication work. No matter how accurately we present our thoughts, nothing will happen if we don't speak each other's languages.

The third option can make effective communication a reality: finding common ground. Everyone is human, which means they share a number of life experiences and emotions. Those similarities can be the touch points that connect people at the heart.

We moved recently, and we haven't met our new neighbors yet. Their work hours are very different than ours, so we haven't happened to be in our driveways at the same time. My wife, Diane, baked some cookies for Christmas, put them in a bag, and added a card. We rang the doorbells of the houses around us, but no one answered. So we hung the bags on our neighbors' doorknobs, hoping to find common ground (everyone has to eat).

A few days later, we found a bag of chocolate truffles hanging from our doorknob, with a handmade card from one of the neighbors. The next day, the college-age son of another neighbor came by to deliver a box of candy from his parents. They evidently speak mostly Japanese and sent him to make the contact. Even though we still haven't had a "formal" conversation, we connected through the common language of caring.

Three Approaches to a Conversation

In the previous chapter, we talked about the filters that influence our conversations. Our unique combination of filters determines what each of us brings to a conversation:

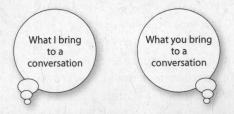

This leads to three approaches to a conversation:

1. Focus on the left circle.

Most people who want to improve their communication skills focus on the left circle. They read books and articles, trying to make their circle bigger. It's a great way to develop a bigger library of topics to discuss. But if they focus solely on the left circle, they'll miss one of the greatest resources to make a conversation work: the experience and perspective of the other person.

2. Focus on the right circle.

In *The Purpose-Driven Life*, Rick Warren begins by saying, "It's not about you."[6] That perspective opens the door for an effective conversation. Most people spend their energy trying to say the right thing, in the right way, and in the right sequence to get the desired response. But if we only focus on what *we* say, we're missing key elements of the conversation: what the *other person* is thinking, feeling, and saying.

This approach recognizes the value of another person's perspective. Exploring another person's experience provides a collection of ingredients that can make a conversation move in new and exciting directions.

Strictly focusing on the perspective of others also fosters a one-sided relationship. And it doesn't help with how to get a conversation started. A third approach makes it easy for anyone to make conversation connections:

3. Focus on the "common ground."

It's tough to make effective conversation by emphasizing either circle over the other. The key is to explore the "overlap"—the common ground where the two circles come together.

The overlap:
"Common
Ground"

That overlap may be tiny or surprisingly large, but it's the place to begin when exploring a new conversation. We don't have to become something we're not; we simply need to find out the common language that both of us speak. As we begin conversing in that area of common experience and interest, we build a foundation for exploring the "unknown edges" of each other's circles. It moves our perspective from "me" to "you" to "us."

If you want to know the people in your neighborhood, you could put up signs to announce your presence. You could hold a barbeque and invite everyone to come. But the easiest way is to find the person you have natural common ground with: your immediate next-door neighbors. You share common property lines and live in close proximity to each other. You share the same fence. One of you might have a tree that drops leaves in the other person's yard. If you have gophers or crabgrass, they probably do, too. It's fairly simple to begin a relationship, since you have so much in common.

Once you get to know them, you get introduced to their neighbor on the other side. Little by little, over time, you get to know the whole block. But it's easier to begin the relationship with your immediate neighbor than to start with the one way down the street.

That's what explorers do. They begin in an area they're familiar with and gradually move into new areas. They're keenly aware of their surroundings, observing the sights and sounds, processing them against what they already know.

The Beauty of Common Ground

All three areas are important. But they're also progressive:

- The left circle (our perspective and what we bring to a relationship) provides the tools for exploring the right circle.
- The right circle (the other person's perspective and what they bring to a relationship) helps us discover what we have in common.
- The overlap (the similarities between our two perspectives) provides the most natural area for conversation to begin.

Focusing on the "common ground" provides a number of specific benefits to effective communication:

It gives you more to talk about.

When you feel like the only one who needs to contribute to a conversation, you have a limited number of "ingredients" to add to the recipe. But looking through another person's perspective is like looking through their kitchen cupboards. They'll have things in their cupboards that you don't, which means you have the potential for preparing dishes you couldn't have imagined before.

It takes the pressure off.

When we only look through our own perspective, we wonder how we are coming across to the other person. But when we attempt to see things through their perspective, we can relax. Genuine interest in others takes energy, which means that energy isn't as available for focusing on ourselves.

It adds adventure.

Quiet personalities often associate words like *terror* and *panic* with making conversation, not *excitement* and *adventure*. But using a simple process that's based on what both people bring to a conversation, the encounter can actually be something they look forward to. Learning the unique experiences of another person can be like traveling to a new country. You may be entering unfamiliar territory, but there's a sense of anticipation because there's so much to see and learn. Once you go, you want to go back.

It takes the guesswork out of a relationship.

Most new relationships are characterized by playing games. We listen to people's words, watch their expressions and gestures and hear their tone of voice, and make assumptions about what they're thinking. But often, we're wrong. Learning to gain another person's perspective provides accurate processing of these conversational dynamics. We don't have to guess what their motives are; we can simply talk about them openly and without defensiveness.

The Dangers of Narrow Focus

When we look at life only from our own perspective, there are two potential problems:

- We feel that we're right, and the other person is wrong.
- We assume that the other person sees things the same way we do.

We feel that we're right and the other person is wrong.

That's a dangerous perspective. If we believe it, we feel like we have to convince the other person to see things our way. But true exploring isn't for the purpose of changing someone's mind; it's for understanding them.

My wife, Diane, is a "doer." When she starts something, she finishes as quickly and thoroughly as possible. In meetings, she will listen for a while and then ask, "OK, what are we going to do, and who's going to be responsible?"

I'm a "thinker." I'm usually seen as an idea person. Give me a problem, and I'll come up with six different possible solutions. I'll come up with things nobody else thinks of. I never actually *do* anything, though; I just dream about doing things.

Shortly after we were married, our different approaches became an issue for us. I thought Diane worked too hard at things and needed to lighten up. On the other hand, it was tough for her to see me brainstorm a number of great ideas but never take any action on them.

Gradually, we came to understand that neither approach was best, just different. The more we worked to understand each other's perspectives, the easier it was to draw from those differences to come up with strong, creative solutions. The more we've explored those perspectives over the years, the stronger our relationship has become.

We assume that the other person sees things the same way we do.

Paula loves a good party. She thought that surprising Jenn on her birthday with a big celebration would be a perfect way to demonstrate her friendship. When Jenn's response was cordial but unenthusiastic, Paula felt hurt and unappreciated.

Phil spent the weekend attending a wedding, having dinner with a group from church, and participating in Sunday activities with extended family. A friend suggested that Phil and his new wife, Barb, join them for coffee on Monday night with several couples. He was looking forward to spending a quiet evening at home, so he politely declined. After renting a movie and buying Chinese take-out, he couldn't understand Barb's disappointment when she found out about the invitation.

Paula and Barb love being surrounded by other people and assume that everyone else does, too. Jenn and Phil don't mind being around people, but it drains their emotional tank pretty quickly.

Both perspectives are real. It's not something that needs to be fixed; it's simply a description of their unique temperament. Ignoring that uniqueness in others puts up a barrier that makes effective communication difficult at best, often impossible.

Moving Forward

"How do I get started? It sounds good, but how do I make those initial connections?"

Keep reading. In the chapters that follow, we'll develop a step-by-step process for starting, maintaining, and ending a conversation.

You'll grow at your own pace. I won't try to change you into someone you're not. I'll make you more of who you already are.

And I promise: You'll enjoy the ride!

PART THREE

Explore
Expectantly

6

Starting a Conversation

When a space shuttle launches, it burns 90 percent of its fuel in the first few minutes to escape the earth's gravity. From that point forward, the fuel consumption drops to a fraction of that original amount.

For many people, starting a conversation is the hardest part of communication. It seems to take 90 percent of our energy just to make the initial contact:

- We don't know how to initiate the interaction.
- We don't know what to say first.
- We don't know if the other person wants to talk to us.
- We don't know how to approach someone.

But once the conversation has started, maintaining the momentum is easier than getting it going in the first place.

An effective conversation begins before the first word is spoken. Both parties go through an unconscious dialogue in their own minds about the accessibility of the other person. We read their body language and facial expressions and interpret those signals to determine the chances for success in approaching them. If we assume the signals are positive, we proceed, cautiously measuring their responses. If we decide the signals are negative, we assume they won't be interested.

But often those assumptions are inaccurate. It's important to separate what we observe from our interpretation of those observations.

While teaching a seminar a few years ago, I observed an older participant in the front row who was obviously disinterested. He would sigh loudly during the class, roll his eyes occasionally, and make no eye contact. His body language and facial expressions seemed to indicate that he would rather be anywhere than in that classroom. I assumed that he had been forced to attend by his manager.

But at the end of the class, he approached me and shook my hand. With no facial expression he said, "Thank you. Best class I've ever attended. Changed my life."

I thought he was joking. But then he continued: "I'm in charge of accounting for this company worldwide. I'm bringing forty-five accountants to Tulsa for a conference in a couple of months. Would you come do this seminar for them?"

Since that time, I've learned to be a little less certain about my assumptions. If a person has his arms crossed, I could assume he's closed and resistant. Sometimes he's just cold.

Challenging Our Assumptions

There are two ways to initiate a conversation:

1. Wait for someone to approach you.
2. Approach someone.

The first approach is the most common for an introvert. They don't want to risk rejection or appear foolish, so they wait for someone to approach. If the other persons take the initiative, the introvert assumes that they find enough interest in them to strike up a conversation. But this approach has some inherent problems:

- If no one approaches them, it reinforces their feelings of inadequacy.
- It puts the focus on themselves instead of the other person.
- They have no control over the outcome.
- It makes the whole process potentially painful.

The second approach is more common for extroverts. They're not as concerned about how they're being perceived, so they are quick to approach others. They assume that everyone is as comfortable in conversation as they are. When it comes to starting a conversation, it's an effective approach.

Quiet people might find the second approach more threatening, so they don't consider it. But the perceived pain usually comes from making certain assumptions:

Assumption #1: "I don't want to intrude."

We assume that if we approach someone, they might be offended. But think about the times you've been approached by someone else; how many times were you offended? In most cases you were grateful that they took the initiative so you didn't have to. If they're standing alone, there's a great chance that they'll welcome the chance to talk. The worst that can happen is that there's no "chemistry," and you can graciously end that conversation and move to someone else. But that's not usually what happens.

Assumption #2: "They might not like me or think I'm interesting."

In this scenario, we assume that our self-talk is accurate. If we see ourselves as boring, we assume that they're thinking: *Oh, great. Look who I'm getting stuck with.* It's true that we form a quick impression when someone approaches us, but the first few seconds of the conversation tell us if we're correct or not. Most people give the benefit of the doubt. They assume that someone approaching them is interesting until they prove otherwise.

Assumption #3: "They're more confident than I am."

Most people try to appear confident and attractive to others, even if they're not feeling that way inside. In most cases, people aren't quite as confident as they appear.

But we all inwardly crave connections. By approaching another person, we're speaking directly to that need. They want conversations to work as much as we do and understand the energy it takes to interact.

Assumption #4: "They're standing alone because they prefer it."

Actually they're doing the same thing we're doing. In a social function, people don't usually stand alone because they don't want to interact. If that were true, they would have stayed home. They're using Option 1 (above), waiting for someone to approach them. If you take the initiative, they'll be relieved.

Assumption #5: "I don't know them, so I don't know what they'd like to talk about."

That assumption is probably true, but it's one of the biggest advantages you have. It takes you off the hook for having to have lots of topics to discuss. You need a few basic exploring tools to get the momentum going, and then you begin searching for ideas in that new territory.

Assumption #6: "I'll feel like a failure if we don't have a great conversation."

That puts all the responsibility on you for a good conversation. Not every interaction has to be great. As you begin to make connections with a variety of people, you'll connect more with some than others. Some connections will be brief and stay on the surface, while others will be extended and dive deeply into each other's lives.

The purpose of conversation isn't to show people how clever you are; it's to make a connection between two people. The outcomes of a conversation don't just say something about you and your conversational skills. They reveal something about the other person as well. It's important to be realistic in how we interpret the results of our interactions.

In a practical sense, here's the greatest advantage of being the one to initiate a conversation: *You get to pick whom you spend time with.*

Where Do I Start?

Years ago I spent time as a radio announcer. One of the best pieces of advice I received from a mentor was that people don't listen to the radio in groups. They listen in their cars or at home, by themselves. If I was going to be successful on the air, I had to hold a conversation with an individual.

So, when you're initiating a conversation, should you start with a group or an individual?

Either one will work. Your ultimate goal is to make a connection with an individual. But approaching a group can be a safe way to make that first contact. Since they're already talking to each other, there's less of a chance that they'll notice you standing alone. So you can "sneak up" on the group and make some observations before deciding to join them.

Grab some snacks and stand close to the group for a couple of minutes. Watch their body language and listen to what they're discussing. The level of their conversation will tell you if this is a group of people who know each other well or if they've just met each other. A group of close friends might form a tight circle to keep intruders away, and they'll discuss issues that have significance only to them. But if they're having a casual conversation about something you have some interest in, stand close enough that someone notices your presence. In most cases, they'll invite you to join them.

If you already know someone in the room, watch to see which group they choose to join. Walk up to them and say, "I don't mean to interrupt, Bob—I just saw you over here and wanted to say 'Hi.' " If you don't know Bob all that well, you might include your name. "Hi, Bob, John Jones; we met in

Dallas, and I just wanted to say hello." At that point Bob will be relieved, because he couldn't quite think of your name, and he'll probably respond by introducing you to the group. If he doesn't, you made a connection and can move to another group.

If you've had a conversation with one person and you know someone else at the event, introduce the two of them. You've simplified the task for them and started a new group. It also makes it easier to exit when appropriate, since they can keep talking without you.

First Words

So you've made your initial entry into a group. What should you say first?

Remember: Your goal is to find common ground. When entering a group, trying to take over the conversation or introduce new topics is not wise. It's safer to pick up on something you've already heard them talking about and make a quick comment or two about it. Comment on something from their perspective rather than your own.

As you enter a group, you hear them discussing the price of gasoline. Don't start by saying, "Well, it's fifty cents higher than that in my neighborhood." Instead, say, "That's a great price. Where do you buy your gas?" If the conversation focuses on the weather, don't start by telling them about the hottest place you've ever lived. Listen long enough to find out what area they're talking about and ask, "Are all of you from that area?" You're "raising the flag" about your thoughts and quickly lowering it, waiting to see if anyone picks up on what you've said. At this point, you're not trying to demonstrate your conversational skills. You're trying to build trust with the people in the group.

Think about groups you've been a part of, when someone broke in and took the dialogue in a whole new direction. If you were in the middle of a conversation, you were frustrated that it ended without warning. Even if no one said anything to the offender, you might have resented them for their lack of sensitivity.

Keep these ideas in mind as you enter a new group:

- Don't begin by talking about yourself. It seems self-serving.

- Don't begin by talking about their opinions. It's risky to comment on anything about someone you've just met. After the initial contact, it's OK to explore, but not initially.

- "Raise the flag" with a comment about the subject they're already discussing. Keep it short, and make sure it's not controversial or opinionated. Your goal is first to build relationships. Once that's done, you've built enough trust to be able to discuss deeper views.

- Be honest. Ask, "Am I intruding?" They'll probably invite you to stay, but be sensitive. If they keep talking about something that's obviously of interest only to them, excuse yourself graciously.

- Don't use sarcasm as an opening remark. It's too risky.

- Don't begin with comments about jobs, sports, health, politics, or religion. This is not the time to convert someone to your point of view. It's time to make a conversational connection that builds trust.

- Use conversational openers that relate to the situation at hand:
  - "So, how do you know [host or hostess]?"
  - "Do you all know each other already?"
  - "Traffic was terrible today. How was it for you?"
  - "What brings you here?"
- Be "in the moment." Block out everything going on around you so you can concentrate on the person you're talking to. It shows respect and keeps your focus on the group members instead of yourself.

Final Approach

After you've spent some time in a group, you'll probably figure out pretty quickly who you're comfortable with and who you're not. Or if you've approached someone directly, you've determined if you want to continue the conversation. It's time to engage that individual.

- Pick up on a comment they made and ask more. People like sharing their opinions.
- Listen for common areas of interest and explore them.
- If they express an opinion you disagree with, don't get defensive. Listen carefully to discover what has led them to feel that way. If you don't mind talking about it, say, "That's interesting. I've always felt differently, but I've never heard your perspective before." Don't get into a debate. You have to build trust first. You might win the debate but lose the relationship. They'll get defensive, and it could actually reinforce their position. They'll find

it refreshing if you care about them as a person, not as a project to convince about something.

- Smile. Genuinely.

- Make eye contact. Don't stare, but make a direct pupil-to-pupil connection.

- Ask their name and use it during the conversation. If it's an unusual name, ask them to pronounce it until you get it right. They'll appreciate the extra effort.

- Ask people to spell their names: "Is it S-a-r-a or S-a-r-a-h?" Since their name is important to them, they'll welcome the sensitivity to get it right. When you introduce them to someone else, say, "This is Sarah, with an *h*."

- Become your own host at the event. Every time you meet a new person, introduce them to someone else.

- If you approach someone who should remember you, assume that they don't. Take the initiative by saying, "Hi, Sheila. Terry Smith. How are you?" You're making their job easier.

- If you forget someone's name, don't pretend to remember it. Just ask. "Tell me your name again . . . ?" You'll both be more comfortable.

What Next?

You've made the initial contact and gotten through the first few moments of a new conversation. Now what?

In the next chapter, we'll learn what to do to keep the conversation going. It's kind of like going on a treasure hunt. In the initial part of the conversation, you're collecting clues. Now you want to search for the treasure. You don't know where it will lead you, but a spirit of exploration can provide stimulating dialogue you might not have thought was possible.

For now, start small. A simple way to practice the ideas in this chapter is to try them in a public place, like a shopping mall or church. Pick ten people, smile, and say, "Good morning." Most will smile back and respond.

That's how easy it is. Once you've gotten comfortable with the initial greeting, begin experimenting with some of the other techniques. The purpose is to make a connection with another person. Every time you try it, your confidence will rise.

7

Developing a Conversation

So you've made contact, and you have their attention. Now what?

It's common to feel self-conscious at this point. You've initiated a conversation, and the other person is looking you in the eye, waiting for you to say something. By approaching someone, you've implied that this will be a valuable conversation. Now it's time to deliver on your promise. What do you say next?

This is exactly the moment when the adventure begins. You're entering new territory and may be moving out of your comfort zone. But if you take the right tools with you, exploring that territory will produce new insights and topics that you've never considered before. The very things you need for "conversational survival" will be found as you explore the new ground.

As you enter a new conversation, you're on the lookout for the common ground between you and another person (as discussed in chapter 5). That common ground becomes your comfort zone with that person. From that foundation, you're ready to begin exploring the other person's territory. This only happens when you change your mind-set from "We won't have anything to talk about" to "We'll find lots of things to talk about."

When I'm teaching a seminar, I make sure I'm set up and ready to go at least an hour ahead of time. That way, I can greet people as they arrive and find "common ground" with them. It's not a gimmick. I genuinely want to know as much as I can about the people I'm spending the day with. This helps me because I can tailor my remarks to their specific needs.

But this helps them as well. I've found that when I spend two or three minutes with someone before a class, they don't feel like they're in a seminar anymore. They feel that they have a basic relationship with me. We're no longer in a teacher/listener role; we're two people working together on common issues. I've often had people comment on the difference those early connections make on their experience.

Tools of the Trade

There are many potential tools, but we'll focus on four essentials here:

- A map and compass
- Binoculars

- A shovel
- Pest repellent

When used effectively, these tools will help you approach any conversation with confidence. They don't guarantee perfection, because you can't control the other person. But they'll give you a process for enjoying the adventure.

Map and Compass (Planning)

Backpackers sit on a mountain peak and study a map to determine where they're headed. They scan the landscape, look for landmarks, and identify the exact direction they need to go. To get to the next peak, however, they have to go through a forested valley where the landmarks aren't visible. Once they've entered the forest, they pull out the compass and follow the route they've already planned.

Too often we go into a conversation without planning and wonder why it doesn't go well. Preparation for a social encounter is like studying a map before beginning the journey. It gives you a sense of where you're heading. Based on that preparation, you'll come up with specific ideas to keep you on track as the conversation progresses. That's your compass; it keeps you moving in the right direction.

How do you prepare for a conversation? By focusing on three things: you, the other person, and the situation you'll be encountering.

- *You*—Most people put all their energy here. If that's your primary focus, you'll weaken your ability to explore. But it's important to prepare a short introduction of yourself.

Develop two "elevator speeches" in case the spotlight turns to you. One should be a thirty-second description of who you are and what you do. The other should do the same thing without mentioning your employment. You'll use the first one often, since people will often begin by asking, "So what do you do?" But the second can open up whole new areas of conversational exploration.

• *The other person*—The same holds true when you focus on the other person. A typical question is, "What do you do?" We assume that it's a good question to find areas of common ground. But it has some inherent risks. The conversation might stay one-dimensional, or the person might drone on endlessly about a technical job that is totally foreign to you. If they're recently unemployed or in a negative job situation, you might create an uncomfortable moment that's hard to recover from.

Try asking questions that have nothing to do with their career. Prepare some of the conversational openers from chapter 6 ahead of time. Think through specific questions you could ask to discover things you would feel comfortable saying about yourself. Write them down to solidify them in your mind.

• *The situation*—A good conversation has a balance of input from both parties. Focusing on either you or the other person risks an imbalance. That's why it's generally safest to focus your comments or questions on either the current situation or outside events that might interest both of you.

Planning ahead is the simplest way to feel comfortable in a new conversation. You wouldn't think of building a house without a blueprint. Why enter a conversation without some advance planning? The time you spend thinking through a potential encounter will give you the tools you need to explore any new situation.

Here are some practical ways you can prepare for your next conversation:

- Think about who you might encounter and a couple of things you could say to them. Write them down.

- Determine if there's anything you already know about them—their interests, hobbies, birthdays, opinions, and background. Ask someone else who knows them for information. If they have a degree of public exposure, a quick Web search could reveal insights about them. This doesn't mean you're becoming a cyber-stalker; you're just finding out as much as you can from public information.

- Read the front page of each section of the newspaper each day to stay current on the things people might be talking about. My wife and I often ask each other about news stories we've heard or who won key sporting events the day before. We know that our clients will be talking about those things, and it's helpful to have a basic knowledge of current events to be able to participate in those conversations.

- Attend any type of event that stretches you and gives you more things to talk about. Take a free class in something or join a club. Attend a city council meeting or read through the minutes online to see what's happening in your community. If you're visiting another community, check out the local section of their newspaper online to see what's happening there.

For making conversation, it's better to know a little about a lot than to be an expert on one thing. You can dive deeply into that one area but will flounder if the other person doesn't have any common ground with you.

Binoculars (Observing)

Larry spent his whole career in law enforcement. He once told me that the thing that set police officers apart from regular citizens was their focus. Most people have their attention captured by whatever is in front of them and ignore everything else. Officers are trained to be aware of what's happening in a situation and not be distracted by what's immediately in front of them.

That often happens in conversation. We're so caught up in making a good impression that we forget to look at the conversational clues all around us. It's a matter of using all of our senses to listen, see, and sense the environment. When we're talking, it's easy to focus on what we're going to say next. Good conversationalists observe the little details and use them for direction.

People tell us what they want to talk about. Listen closely and you'll hear snippets of things they're volunteering to explore with you. They're giving you information about the landscape.

When they're responding to a question, listen for things in their answers beyond what was asked. Those are clues about things they are willing to explore. For example, you ask where they grew up. They respond, "Oh, mostly on the East Coast. But since my dad was military, we moved around a lot." You've just been given some clues to follow up on:

- "What branch of the service was he in?"
- "In what other places did you live?"
- "So when you think about growing up, where do you consider home?"
- "How often did you move?"
- "What was it like as a kid having to start your life over every few years?"

A few weeks ago I spoke in a class at a church in Bakersfield. When I met the associate pastor who was in charge of the class, I listened for clues to find common ground. I found out that he had formerly been an executive pastor in Phoenix, where I grew up. That led to a brief conversation about sports, since both of us were fans of the Phoenix Suns basketball team. It was a short conversation, but we could have talked about the heat in Phoenix, the price of real estate, or the rapid growth of the city. Those things are common ground for anyone from Phoenix.

Being observant makes it easy to design simple questions around areas of common interest.

- At a wedding, ask, "How do you know the bride/groom?"
- At a conference, ask, "What brought you to this convention?"
- With someone who's recovering from surgery, ask, "Where does it hurt the *least*?" (I used this with someone once, who said it was the most refreshing thing she had been asked.)

Observe body language to know what's going on. Most body language is subconscious, so it's a good reflection of what a person is really feeling and thinking. Eye contact, gestures, and movement can give hints as to how a conversation is progressing. Introverts often give good eye contact when listening but look away when speaking. Extroverts might connect well with their eyes when they're speaking, because they're focused. But if they listen for a long time without being able to say anything, their eyes tend to drift. If we don't understand those realities, we can mistakenly assume that someone isn't paying attention when they are genuinely connecting with what we're saying.

Pick up on things in the environment. A logo on a sweatshirt or a unique piece of jewelry can be a starting point for discussion. Look for pictures and decorations in a home or office that indicate a person's values and experiences. Try it right now. Look around you. What are the things you see that you could bring up in conversation?

A sincere compliment builds a bridge between people that opens up warm communication. It makes them feel good about you for observing, makes them feel good about themselves, and makes them more open to conversation. Compliment the things you notice that genuinely impress you: their home, decorations, food. Point out things you notice that they do well, such as their ability to talk with clients and guests, and make them feel comfortable and safe in conversation.

Shovel (Digging)

Once you've made enough observations about your environment to have some topics to discuss, it's time to dig deeper. It's simply a matter of choosing which new path to follow and exploring for a while. If that path doesn't lead anywhere, you can always try another.

Think of this as a treasure hunt. If you're patient and explore carefully, there's a good chance you'll find a wealth of information, as well as the potential for a solid connection with another person.

Start with a mind-set of genuine curiosity. Instead of worrying about how a conversation is going, focus on finding out what the other person knows that you don't. Everyone is an expert in something; they've had life experiences or knowledge that you haven't discovered. Make it your goal to find out what those things are.

Restate the things they're telling you in your own words; it shows your interest. This can be easily done with a comment such as, "So, let me see if I got this straight. You . . ." As you learn about their unique experiences, the door will be open for you to share comments about your own experiences.

There's a fine balance between focusing on them and talking about yourself. You want to contribute, but you don't want to appear arrogant or monopolize the conversation. But every healthy conversation involves participation from both people. If it's one-sided, it will be less satisfying over time than if both people get to contribute.

When you do talk about yourself, don't dive too deeply. It's one thing to be candid. But with someone you've just met, you need to build trust before exposing your inner secrets.

One of the best ways to explore is to ask questions. You can plan them ahead of time, and they can be powerful during a conversation if they focus on things the other person has brought up. Questions are a great tool, so we'll spend all of chapter 13 on them.

Pest Repellent (Preventing Problems)

Any trip can be ruined by bugs. No matter how striking the scenery is, you'll be miserable if you're swatting mosquitoes all day. A good insect repellent can make the difference in the success of a trip.

In conversation, there are some "bugs" that can spoil the experience. The good news is that by recognizing them and avoiding them, we have a much greater potential for enjoying the encounter.

- Don't express controversial opinions too early after meeting someone. If they disagree, they'll become defensive. It takes time to build enough trust to share at this level. Build the trust first, and you'll earn the right to be heard.

- Try to avoid talking about work in the early stages of a conversation. That way both people can learn about each other outside of their professions.

- Make it a two-sided conversation. Explore the other person's experience, but then contribute from your own.

- Don't tell jokes. If you don't know someone well, you won't know what might offend them. Humor, which is simply taking a light view of life, is acceptable. Jokes are too risky.

- Don't try to pretend you're something you're not. The more integrity you have between your inner and outer self, the stronger foundation you'll be building for a genuine friendship.

Worth the Effort

When a new ride opens at Disneyland, the waiting lines can be hours long. We all want to see the new attraction, and we're willing to wait. Once we've ridden the ride, we're glad we did. We have new experiences to talk about that make life richer.

Conversations enrich our lives. Other people have different perspectives and life experiences. As we draw them out in conversation, we can anticipate learning new perspectives to add to our own.

Last week I stayed at a hotel in Del Mar, California. As I left my room, a woman from the housekeeping staff was placing newspapers in front of each guest room door. She was carrying several dozen papers, so I commented that she wouldn't need to exercise that day. She responded with a smile and told me about her one-year-old son whom she picks up throughout the day—her "personal weight-lifting" program. As we talked, it was obvious that she wasn't used to hotel guests engaging her in conversation. Entering the elevator, I realized that this short encounter brightened both of our days.

I'm guessing that we were both in a better mood that day because of caring conversation, which carried over to the other people we met throughout our day. By engaging people in genuine, connective conversation, we offer them grace to face the challenges of their lives.

Conversations don't have to be lengthy to be successful. In the next chapter, we'll talk about the signs that tell you a conversation is running out of steam so you can end it while there is still energy around it.

8

Ending a Conversation

It takes a lot of work to start a conversation—overcoming hesitancy, approaching someone, checking our mind-set, and saying the right things. It also takes a lot of energy to keep a conversation going well. That's where we usually put our focus. So it's surprising to most people that ending a conversation can often be the toughest part.

Conversations usually end in two ways: a satisfying conclusion or a painful escape. In a healthy, enjoyable conversation, simple skills can leave each party feeling positive about the encounter. In a conversation that just isn't working, there are ways to escape that can keep both parties from feeling that the conversation was a waste of time.

We've all been trapped in conversations that weren't working. Why is it such a discouraging experience? Let's look at the reasons we stay in conversation longer than we should and talk about when and how to make our exit.

Why We Stay Too Long

It seems like it would be obvious when a conversation begins to drag. But in the middle of the conversation, we might be so focused on keeping it going that we overlook some of the common signals that it's time to end the interaction:

1. *The conversation is going well.* This reflects a mind-set that says, "If it ain't broke, don't fix it." Every good, energetic conversation can take a downward turn when you begin to exhaust the topics (or each other). The best time to finish is when things are going well, so you'll leave wanting to spend more time together in the future. If you wait too long, you'll end the conversation on a note of low energy. Both of you will think, *OK, that's enough.*

   It's better to leave on a high note. Leaving a conversation if you're enjoying it is hard, but you can always come back after making other connections.

2. *We don't know how to escape without being rude.* No matter how badly the conversation may be going, most people hesitate to be rude. So they feel trapped in an uncomfortable situation without the resources to find a way out.

3. *We're afraid of moving on to another conversation.* After all, we invested a lot of emotional energy to get the conversation to this point. Why go through that process all over again?

   Don't forget that you're trying to develop your conversational skills, as well as explore the rich life experiences of others. If you settle in when you get comfortable, you'll miss the chance to practice your skills and explore other opportunities.

4. *We lose control of a conversation.* Occasionally, we connect with someone who uses a conversation for their own therapeutic purposes. Most people ask, "How was your weekend?" The response is typically, "Good. How was yours?" But sometimes people launch into a ten-minute monologue of their entire weekend, including details you really don't want to hear. When that happens, it's difficult to pry yourself away. When people are baring their soul, we don't want to come across as uncaring (even if it's true in that case).

Recently, I sent emails to two different friends whom I haven't had contact with for years. The messages were only two or three sentences long, asking basic questions about how they've been doing and what they're up to. In both cases their printed replies filled four or five single-spaced pages, detailing everything that's happened in their lives over the past decade. I care deeply about both of them. But I felt as if they'd been hungry for someone to listen to them for years, and the floodgates opened when they got a listening ear.

My first thought was relief that I wasn't talking to them in person. My second feeling was guilt for feeling that way. But I realized that I wasn't being rude or uncaring. I just needed to learn appropriate boundaries and techniques for staying in control of those conversations and bringing them to an appropriate conclusion.

From Success to Excess

We sometimes have a tendency to feel that we're not successful if every conversation doesn't go well. But if our standard is perfection, we'll be disappointed every time.

Why? Making conversation is a dynamic process, so every encounter is different. As carefully as we might choose our responses, we can't control the other person. Every conversation will be different, and some will go better than others. Comparing each conversation with a standard of perfection is unrealistic. Instead, we need to look at each conversation as a unique interaction that can hone our conversational skills, provide new insight into another person's experience, and add richness to our life experience.

Every conversation won't be "great." Expect this. It's OK.

Salespeople recognize that rejection is part of the job. They learn from those experiences and use them to strengthen their efforts in the future. When a conversation doesn't go well, it doesn't simply describe your performance; it says something about the other person as well. We can't evaluate our abilities based on someone else's performance.

For example, some people won't respond well despite your best efforts. They could be too shy or have significant life issues that are getting in the way of interacting with you. Staying in those conversations will be frustrating for you and disappointing for them. In those situations it's best to end a conversation politely, give them something positive to encourage them, and move on.

If a conversation isn't working, it's OK to end it. That's why you want to think through strategies for ending it ahead of time.

The Great Escape

Ending isn't always such a bad thing. In fact, every conversation has to end sometime. So how do you do it gracefully?

The greatest resource you have is *preparation*. If you enter every conversation with a clear sense of where you're headed and what you want to accomplish, you have a much greater chance of a fulfilling connection.

It's like a global positioning system (GPS) in your car. You enter the address of your destination. Using data from satellites, the GPS determines your current location and uses it to get you to your destination. If you make a wrong turn, the GPS refigures the route based on your new location. But everything is based on having entered the destination.

The same is true with conversation. If you have a clear understanding of your purpose for the conversation, you'll be able to keep the interaction on track when it begins to take a detour. Your purposes might include:

- Meeting new people
- Practicing your conversational skills
- Learning new information
- Networking for business purposes
- Asking for a favor
- Selling a product or service
- Enjoying interaction with other people
- Convincing someone to take a course of action
- Motivating another person to consider an option
- Encouraging someone who needs a lift

Once you have a clear sense of your purpose, use the following skills for graciously ending a conversation:

- *Practice conversational "martial arts."* When I was a kid, judo was the primary form of self-defense that people learned. The appeal was that you didn't have to be strong to defend yourself. If someone was rushing to attack you, you would simply learn to redirect that oncoming energy, and the attacker would end up on the floor. When someone is forcefully moving a conversation along an uncomfortable path, you can redirect that energy into a new direction to take control of the conversation again.

  In the locker room of a gym recently, a person standing near me was expressing strong opinions about a news item on the overhead television. His forceful approach made me uncomfortable, and I really didn't feel equipped to debate his views. Instead, I deflected his comments to go a new direction: "Yeah, it seems like there are a lot of stories like that on the news lately. When was the last time you saw something on the news that was encouraging instead of depressing?" His tone changed, and he began responding without realizing he had been moved in a new direction.

- *Be honest.* Don't make excuses for why you want to end the conversation. Think about the most interesting parts of your conversation, acknowledge them, and use them to make your exit.

  For example: "I've never really talked to anyone who has been bungee jumping before. I don't think I'd want to try it, but it's been fascinating hearing your experience. I've got a number of other people I want to connect with before this evening is over, so I need to scoot. Thanks for talking—enjoy your evening." It's gracious and direct and doesn't leave room for negotiation. You've simply stated what you're going to do and encouraged them along the way.

- *Make the exit about you.* If you've clearly defined your purpose before the event, you can use that as a legitimate tool for exiting a conversation. You can simply tell the person that you're going to do something, or talk to someone, or be someplace, or see something. The other person sees that you're trying to accomplish what you came for, not just trying to escape them.

  If you do that, make sure you do what you said you were going to do. If you leave because you wanted to talk to the host, don't get sidetracked along the way by a different conversation. The person you left will notice and see you as dishonest. If you only use it as an excuse but have no intention of talking to the host, you'll find yourself alone. That can start the negative self-talk again, and you'll have trouble initiating another conversation or entering another group.

- *Ask for their help in accomplishing your purpose.* At some point in the conversation, let them know what you're trying to accomplish. Ask if they have any expertise in a certain subject or know someone in the room who does. This will give them a sense of partnership as they help you reach your goal.

  Here's an example: "Do you know anyone who has started a small business from the ground up? I'm researching that right now and would love to meet someone who has done it." If the person you're talking to knows the subject, you can explore that area more thoroughly. If not, they will be inclined to direct you to someone who might fit that description. If they don't know anyone in that category, you can excuse yourself to continue your search.

- *Take advantage of group dynamics.* Next time you're at a social function, watch what happens when a small group of people is talking. If one or two people walk up and join the group, one or two others will use that as a chance to move away from that group. There's no clear explanation for their behavior, but you can take advantage of that reality.

  Watch the dynamics of the group you're in. If someone joins the group, it's a natural time to slip away unobtrusively. Of course, it won't work if no one joins your group. That's when it's time to utilize one of the other strategies.

  The other dynamic is that when someone begins to monopolize a group conversation, people find ways to exit graciously. When you see that happening, make sure you're not the last person to leave. You'll find yourself in an uncomfortable one-on-one conversation that might be hard to escape.

- *Help people meet each other.* If you've already met a couple of people in a social setting, try introducing them to each other. Point out their areas of common interest so they can begin a conversation. As they make eye contact and begin connecting, excuse yourself politely and move on. They'll appreciate not having to do the hard work of initiating, and you'll have a way to keep things moving.

  I use this technique almost daily. As seminar participants arrive, I spend a few minutes getting to know each one. When I find two people who live in the same area, work in the same field, or have something else in common, I introduce them. It's not a manipulative technique. I'm actually facilitating the flow of conversation by acting as an informal host for the event. People will appreciate efforts such as these when they experience the benefits.

I've found that this is the best way to develop a sense of community in a group. Make sure you do this for the right motives. If you do it simply to get rid of a boring person, the one you introduce them to will resent you for putting them in that situation.

Knowing your purpose and being prepared provides you with the tools you'll use to be in control of whom you talk to and how long you converse.

Achieving a Smooth Finish

During a conversation, it's natural to be focused on your performance, your appearance, and how the other person is responding. But realize that they're doing the same thing. Most people are thinking of themselves more than the other person. This sounds negative and selfish, but it's realistic. Thinking of yourself is a strategy for personal survival. Recognize that both people are doing it to some degree, and it will minimize the pressure to perform.

People remember their first impressions and their last impressions. That's why it's important to end a conversation with strength. Don't drag a conversation down by waiting too long to end it. Practice a variety of strong endings and use them appropriately. Don't just "fade out" from a conversation; make it an event. Shake hands, make eye contact, and end with a comment about why you valued the conversation:

- "Well, it's been great to talk with someone who knows so much about (subject). Thank you."
- "Thanks for the insights about (subject). I appreciate you sharing with me. Here's what I think I'll do with this information . . ."

Ending strong leaves you with a good feeling and helps the other person leave feeling better about themselves. Make it your goal to serve the other person. After they spend time with you, they should feel better about both of you.

After you end a conversation, take time to reflect on what you are walking away with. What do you have now because of that conversation that you didn't have when it started? New information? A contact for future opportunities? The joy of a successful connection with another person?

That's when you know a conversation has been successful: you both feel rewarded for the effort.

9

After a Conversation

Hiking in a remote area, you come across a cave. You enter cautiously and begin to explore. Your flashlight reflects off small glassy spots on the wall, so you approach for a closer look. Your investigation reveals that you've discovered a diamond mine. From your experience, you realize how rich that mine is. So you chip out a few stones, put them in your bag, and exit.

An expert looks at the stones and confirms that they are unequaled in quality. Your wealth has increased dramatically. If you return to the mine, you'll increase your wealth immeasurably.

Would you go back? Or would you be satisfied with the diamonds you collected on your first trip?

Obviously, you'd make the return trip. You wouldn't want to leave that kind of potential untouched. To make sure you could find the mine again, you would probably scribble down anything that would pinpoint the location: landmarks, direction of the sun, and details about the landscape. You would draw a map, take pictures, and use your global positioning unit if you had one available. As soon as possible, you'd go back to the mine again, seeking the richness it had to offer.

Conversations are like that. We might enjoy the encounter and even discover nuggets of wealth from our time together. But that's often where it ends. Most conversations end when two people quit talking and walk away from each other. But that overlooks a valuable opportunity to mine treasures in that same relationship in the future.

Sales professionals know that it's easier and less costly to retain a current customer than to recruit a new one. That's true in conversations as well; it's easier to build on one you've had than to start a new one. In many cases, following up a conversation can be an ongoing source of satisfaction and fulfillment for both people involved in the process.

Why Revisit the Mine?

Extroverts tend to want as many relationships as possible. Since they derive their energy from social connections, they thrive on having a number of people in their lives. For them, it's called networking. They'll use a current conversation as a launching pad to reach other people. Following up on these conversations can provide an exponential increase in the number of people they can connect with.

But even with that potential, they often focus on the conversation they're having with no thought to reconnecting in the future. They're so excited about finding diamonds that they put their energy into finding more diamond mines, pulling a few stones out of each one. They're good at exploring but miss the opportunities that are directly in front of them.

It's different for an introvert. They prefer fewer, deeper relationships. Initiating and holding a conversation is rewarding but drains their energy. By treating each encounter as a one-time event, they're robbing themselves of the very thing that could make the process less stressful.

Revisiting a conversation provides a number of benefits:

- You don't have to go through the process of starting a new conversation as often.
- You can form deeper relationships with the people you encounter.
- It's nonthreatening because you've already gotten to know the person.
- You're developing a network of people you already know, who can introduce you to others.
- In a work environment, you become more visible and influential as you strengthen personal ties.

Regardless of their personality style, most people put their energy into a conversation and ignore the treasure that is available through follow-up. Tapping the potential of repeated connections can lead to a lifetime of satisfying, fulfilling conversation.

Dig Your Well Before You're Thirsty

Following up on conversations is a simple, nonthreatening process. During the conversation, you'll be exploring for information you can use for future connections. After the conversation, you'll organize that information for quick access.

As you're interacting with someone, ask yourself if this is a person you'd like to have contact with again. If so, begin setting the environment for follow-up before the conversation ends:

- Remember that your first conversation is like peeling an onion. It starts on the surface and gradually goes deeper and deeper in future conversations. If you try to go too deep before trust has developed, the other person might feel defensive or threatened. Peeling off one layer during the first meeting gives you a natural place to start on your second meeting.

- Think about how connected you feel when someone expresses their appreciation for you. You'll remember their words of affirmation years later. It's human nature to enjoy such encouragement, so offer it honestly in conversation. Find something about their personality, style, or accomplishments that you admire and tell them. If your compliment is genuine, it will make them want to connect with you again in the future.

- Focus on the "overlap" between your two circles of life experience. That's where you'll have the greatest chance of connecting again in the future, because it's an area of common interest. You're entering into their world, and they're entering into yours. That overlap begins to grow, which provides fertile ground for further exploration.

- Repeat their name during the conversation. People appreciate hearing the sound of their own name, and it's a simple way to establish a quick, caring bond between two people. Don't overdo it, though. Using someone's name a few times makes a positive connection between you and them. Using it too often will come across as an artificial technique.

- Pay close attention to the topics you've discussed to see if there might be an opportunity to build on them later. When the second conversation occurs, make sure you refer to those things.

- Listen for hints about their preferred communication style. If they repeatedly mention talking to people on the phone, they'll probably be open to a call from you a few weeks later reminding them of your conversation. If they primarily mention receiving emails, they're letting you know that they prefer you to contact them in writing. This may not be your favorite way to connect, but it's theirs. You'll build trust when you use their personality style to communicate rather than just your own.

- If they express interest in something you're talking about, offer to get more information to them in a few days. That gives you a valid invitation to make another contact with them. "I'll be glad to get you that information. Where can I drop it off, and what would be a good time?" If they hesitate at a personal meeting, offer to send the information by mail or email if appropriate. At the agreed upon time and place, make the follow-up contact (after preparing for that encounter as well).

- If you're talking with them at a regularly scheduled meeting or social event, ask if they're planning to come to the next one. Jot the person's name and topical reminders on your calendar for the date of the next event so you'll be prepared when it occurs.

- If it's appropriate at the end of a conversation, ask directly if they'd like to meet again. Suggest a "common ground" activity that you both enjoy. Don't suggest something you haven't talked about, such as bowling or sushi. They might not like either. Keep your suggestion simple. People will be more inclined to meet casually at Starbucks with a new acquaintance than to commit to having dinner or attending a theatrical event. That comes a few layers deeper on the onion.

- If they decline, make it easy for them. Don't ask why; just thank them and end the conversation. But send them a short, honest "It was great to meet you" note the next day, just to keep the connection.

When I'm leading a seminar, participants often ask if they can call me later to talk about the ideas they've heard. As an introvert, I find talking on the phone pretty draining. It's much easier for me to talk with people face-to-face or in writing. I really don't mind responding to emails from these people, because I can edit my responses before sending them as well as control when I take care of them.

Knowing that these invitations will happen, I've prepared a simple, direct response: "I'd love the chance to connect about your questions. Email works best for me. Here's my email address. If you want to drop me a note, I'll be happy to 'chat' electronically." This is a direct, positive response and doesn't leave room for negotiation.

Introverts often feel out of control on the phone, so email becomes a very satisfying way to follow up a conversation. It also allows you to keep your phone number private if you prefer. Occasionally, these email conversations lead to meeting again in person. But you get to decide.

How to Relocate the Treasure

If you really had discovered a huge diamond mine, you'd make sure you did everything you could to find it again. In the same way, one of the most important things you can do after a conversation is to find a way to organize your thoughts for follow-up later.

Does that mean taking notes? In most cases, yes. Writing down the things you learned while exploring another person's life is one of the best ways to prepare for future conversations. Organizing that information in a way that's easy to retrieve will provide resources for confident communication the next time you meet.

"But that sounds manipulative and artificial. If I really cared about the person, I would just remember. I wouldn't have to write stuff down, right?"

Albert Einstein was considered to be one of the smartest men in the world. A reporter once asked him for his phone number. Einstein went to the phone directory, looked it up, and wrote it down. When asked why he didn't know his own number, he replied, "Why should I memorize something when I know where to find it?" He saved his mental energy for more important things.

Most of us have had a detailed conversation with someone and were embarrassed in a later conversation with them when we didn't remember any of it. If we had taken the time to jot a few notes about the conversation, we could have reviewed them before beginning that second interaction. Note-taking is simply a tool to help us perform an important task. Like any tool, it does certain things better than we can. We use tools to do jobs more easily. It's not a sign of weakness to admit you can't remember details.

Taking notes after a conversation and organizing them might seem fake or manipulative. But trying to remember details takes mental energy. That means that energy is no longer available to work on the task at hand. In fact, research has shown that one of the primary causes of stress is trying to keep everything in your head. If you write something down where it will be available when you need it, you've actually earned the privilege of forgetting it.

When you know you're going to have a conversation with someone you've spoken with before, a quick review of the key points puts you back on common ground quickly when the conversation begins. They'll be impressed when you remember things they discussed with you before, which demonstrates to them that you paid attention during their initial conversation.

You may ask, "But isn't it dishonest to pretend you remember something when you really had to look it up?" You're not trying to hide your technique. If they ask how you remembered, just tell them the truth. They will be impressed that you have the information, no matter where it came from. Even if you took it from your notes, people are just as impressed that you cared enough about their conversation to keep track of what they said. Whether from memory or written records, people feel cared about when you've invested in the process.

I've learned to just be honest about my note-taking. When I bring up details from a conversation a year earlier, the person usually says, "Wow! Good memory. I'm impressed!" I respond with, "Don't be. I just take good notes." The impact is the same, and the conversation continues on a different level.

A woman I work with leaves me a voice mail every year on my birthday. I don't see her often, but she has called faithfully for the past twelve years. I know she has a list of people she calls, and it doesn't bother me that she needs a list to help her remember. In fact, she called about a week late last year, and I remember how disappointed I was until I finally heard from her. When I asked her about it, she was honest: "I got a new copy of the corporate list, and it was set up differently. So I didn't see your name in time." I still felt just as appreciated, knowing that she took the time to call at all.

There are some people whose special days I remember without reminders. I send an email to friends like Doug and Sandy on their anniversary without having to look it up, and Marlene gets a birthday greeting the same way. Family members are in my head. But for most people, I need those calendar reminders.

We had lunch this weekend with my wife's parents. The discussion moved toward details of their grandchildren and numerous great-grandchildren. When we got into details of their birthdays, graduation dates, ages, and other specifics, they had to work harder to keep track. Finally, they pulled out a calendar. That doesn't mean they don't care; it simply means they have too many details to keep track of without the help of tools.

Whatever method you use must fit your personality, but it has to be simple. Generally, you want to keep each person's information on a single page, and then file the pages alphabetically. Don't file them by date, because you won't remember when you talked with someone a year after a conversation. But when they call and give you their name, you can quickly grab their information if it's filed alphabetically.

Some people use index cards, while others use individual pages. Software such as Outlook, Lotus Notes, or ACT provides a field for notes with each individual in your contact list. After a conversation, jot down any key information you discovered, including:

- family information
- special interests
- major events
- hobbies
- special dates
- areas of common ground you discussed
- length of employment
- where they have lived
- birthplace

I use a small binder with half-sized sheets. I put the person's contact information at the top and file the sheet behind alphabetical tabs. If the person gives me a business card, I staple it to the top of the sheet. That notebook stays on my desk, so it's immediately available when someone calls. If I'm going to meet someone for lunch, I can review the information before leaving my office.

Recently, I've started using the contact field in Outlook for the same information. I haven't decided if I'm going to move more in that direction or not. It really doesn't matter, as long as the information is accessible.

At the end of a conversation, you might exchange business cards with someone. If you do, take a moment as soon as you can to jot notes on the back of the card. We think we'll remember details of a conversation later, but it's almost impossible to keep track of people in that way.

I learned this a few years ago after a conversation with Dr. Howard Hendricks of Dallas Theological Seminary. A few weeks later I received a note that said, "I found your card in my coat pocket. I'm sure I asked for it so I could send you something—but I have no idea what it was. Usually I write it down, but I forgot. What do I need to send you?" I didn't feel bad that he didn't remember. In fact, I felt affirmed that he took the time to follow up and do what he promised.

Maximize Your Efforts

It seems like it could take a lot of time and effort to do this kind of preparation before a conversation and to follow up afterward. But it's only a fraction of the time, energy, and stress it takes to start a new conversation from scratch. Going back to the same diamond mine takes time but produces great rewards. Most people spend time trying to find new mines instead of working the mines they already have.

I'm not suggesting you set up a spreadsheet to keep track of all your contacts, making the whole process mechanical. It's just about investing a few minutes before and after a conversation to maximize the impact of your time together. The time you take to think through your own process could be the key to turning conversations into satisfying relationships for both people involved.

PART FOUR

Focus
Outwardly

10

Learning to Listen

Laura and Ben followed the open house signs dotting the roads on a Saturday afternoon, hoping to find a new place that would meet their needs. In one house, the agent described the features of the construction, when it was built, and what kind of school district it was in. He talked about the number of kids in the neighborhood and the opportunities to connect with growing families. But he never took the time to listen to Laura and Ben's needs. Had he done so, he would have discovered that they were childless. They probably wouldn't have discussed their painful struggles with infertility. But if he had taken the time to listen to them, he would have had the chance to view them as people and not just a potential sale.

We've all been in those situations where we knew that a salesperson was more interested in closing the deal than genuinely meeting our needs. We've also been in conversations where we did most of the talking and the other person did most of the listening. They didn't say much at all, but we walked away thinking, "Wow! That person is a great conversationalist." The encounter stands out in our minds when it occurs because we're not used to it. Listening tends to be a lost art but can be a powerful tool for making connections with others.

When I was a seminary student in the mid-seventies, a classmate carried out an experiment for a class assignment. He put an ad in the local paper that said, "Will listen without interrupting for one hour. $50." He was hoping to get a few calls from people who would simply give their reactions to his unusual approach. But before the experiment was over, he made about $600.

A therapist friend calls this "guided listening." Some of his clients are starved to have someone listen to them and are willing to pay for someone to do so in a structured setting.

For most of us, listening wasn't given much attention as we were growing up. Think about how much time you spent learning to read. Your parents introduced you to books; you had assignments in school; you might have even taken a speed-reading course as an adult. The same is true with writing and speaking. We had formal instruction throughout our school days about how to write effectively and had to make presentations in front of a class to develop our speaking skills.

How much formal instruction did you have on how to listen?

For most of us the answer is "none." It's one of the most powerful communication skills, but it hasn't been taught. Someone has said that God gave us two ears and one mouth, which shows the proportion that we should be using them.

Talk show host Larry King said, "I never learn anything while I'm talking. I realize every morning that nothing I say today will teach me anything, so if I'm going to learn a lot today, I'll have to do it by listening."[7]

Are You a Good Listener?

How do you rate as a listener? When you're in a conversation:

- Do you find yourself planning your reply when the other person is talking?
- Do you tend to interrupt people with your thoughts and reactions before they've finished their thoughts?
- Do you get impatient when someone takes too long to explain something?
- Do you feel more of a need to get your point across than to understand their perspective?
- Do you tend to give advice when people share their struggles with you?
- Do people often say that you're a good listener?

Your honest answers to these questions can indicate your listening skills. If your answers focus mostly on others, you've learned the value of listening and probably look forward to any suggestions that can help you improve. If your answers focus mostly on yourself, you're on the verge of learning something that could dramatically change the effectiveness of your conversations.

The Impact of Listening

When people feel listened to, they feel comfortable and want to make a connection with the other person. When they don't feel listened to, they don't develop trust with that person.

That's true in business. If you don't listen to customers they'll go somewhere else. They might even pay more for an item somewhere else just because they didn't connect with you. This is especially important in certain professions, such as hairstyling or consulting. People are paying to spend several hours with you and won't repeat the experience if you don't listen.

When someone doesn't listen to us, it feels like they're saying, "I'm not interested in you, and I really don't care. I'm more interested in me." That statement might not be accurate, but it's the message that comes across. The person might feel like they're asking the right questions, not interrupting, and doing their best to connect in a conversation. But if we don't feel like they're listening, it doesn't matter.

When we don't feel that the other person is listening, we don't feel a bond with that person. Since trust hasn't developed we don't feel connected. Without making a connection, the chances of that relationship progressing are pretty slim.

How Can You Tell When Someone Is Not Listening?

If everyone had a television monitor on their forehead that displayed exactly what they were thinking, it would be easy to tell when someone had tuned out of a conversation. Since that's not possible, we have to rely on our senses to observe what's happening. Somehow, we just sense when someone isn't listening. What are the signals we pick up on that indicate their lack of interest?

Many studies have been done, and the results vary. But all of them point to the same conclusion: When body language and facial expressions don't match what's being said, we tend to believe those physical signals over the verbal ones. One of the earliest studies showed that only 7 percent of communication takes place through our words. Thirty-eight percent comes through the tone of voice, while 55 percent comes through our body language.[8]

We can fake our words, but it's hard to fake body language. When we're talking to someone, we're using our senses to take in information about what's happening. We hear the words, but we're watching their actions. Consciously or unconsciously, we pick up signals that indicate someone isn't listening:

- They don't maintain good eye contact.
- They nod and respond but never engage with the topic or ask for details.
- They respond inappropriately to what you were just discussing (their reply doesn't match the topic).
- Their facial expression is blank.
- Their body language indicates they're not interested in your ideas.
- Their eyes glaze over while you're talking, even while making eye contact.
- They're easily distracted by movements behind you.
- They hear the first few things you bring up and then start telling you what you should do about the situation.

While we might not be conscious of these signals, our subconscious picks them up. The result is that we don't connect with the other person.

It goes both ways. When we give off these signals to someone else, they feel the same way and fail to connect. "But that's not what I meant," you say. It doesn't matter, because their perception is their reality. Those little signals help them form an impression of you, right or wrong.

One problem is that we can take in information faster than we can deliver it. So while someone is talking at a certain speed, we listen at a faster speed. That makes it possible to multitask when we're listening, letting our mind wander in many different directions. We think that goes unnoticed, but the other person's subconscious is forming a perspective about us.

Ways to Improve Your Hearing

During a conversation, the person you're talking to is wondering, "I wonder if she is really interested in what I'm saying." They'll get their answer by watching your conversational signals. Saying the right things helps them see your interest and makes them want to continue talking. Giving the right signals tells them that they can trust you and makes them want to keep the connection going. If we're aware of those signals and understand them, we can monitor them. It's not a manipulative technique but a way of making sure that our nonverbal signals don't get in the way of effective conversation.

As you become more aware of what's happening in your conversations, look for the signals you're sending to the person with whom you're talking:

- Ask questions based on what they talk about and then listen carefully to their reply instead of thinking about what you're going to say next. By listening carefully, you'll get information from their response that provides new directions for the conversation.

- Learn to consciously tune out everything else that's going on around you. You've probably been around a few people who do that, and it's pretty impressive. It says, "You're so important that the things happening around us don't distract me." It can be tough to do when distractions increase. But practice makes perfect and helps you form a genuine connection with people. Pretending there is no one else in the room takes conscious effort. If someone calls your name, give them a brief wave to indicate that you'll be with them in a few minutes. Then continue your conversation. If appropriate, you might ask them to join your conversation, which keeps the other person included while helping build their network.

- Maintain good eye contact. Someone has called effective eye contact an "emotional handshake" and "looking in the windows of the soul." Nothing makes you connect better than good eye contact, and nothing damages a potential relationship more quickly than when it is ignored.

  My wife and I learned this shortly after we were married. She is great at multitasking and can hold deep conversations while cleaning the kitchen cupboards. But I couldn't talk about sensitive issues unless she was giving me eye contact. Today we both have learned to multitask if it's a benign issue but sit down together over coffee for a serious discussion.

- Use all of your senses (eyes, ears, mind, and heart) to be aware of the signals you're giving or receiving. If you're consciously aware of what's going on, you'll be able to pick up the dynamics that are happening below the surface.

- Nod occasionally to let people know you're listening. You're not necessarily nodding to show agreement. You're acknowledging that you're with them and you're hearing what they're saying.

- Don't interrupt. Usually we interrupt without thinking because we just thought of something we want to drop into the conversation. But if the person isn't finished, they'll feel like you didn't value what they were saying as much as what you wanted to say.

- Don't be afraid of silence. It's like a conversational vacuum; the longer it lasts, the more we feel like we have to say something. Silence can feel like the breakdown of the conversation is becoming obvious, implying that we don't have enough conversational skills to keep it going. But if you allow silence long enough to let them speak first, they'll give you more information to build on. Salespeople have learned the value of waiting. They get information that they probably couldn't get in any other way.

- When you're going to add your own comment, relate it to what they've just said. Draw from their perspective and then add your own, which demonstrates the fact that you've heard what they were saying.

- Restate what you've just heard them say. Don't just parrot it; they'll think you're using some psychological gimmick on them. Summarize in your own words what they were just discussing and ask them if you understand it accurately. It takes a significant level of listening to do this so they'll feel understood. This is an especially good approach when someone is upset about something. When they feel understood, it provides a way for them to release that emotion.

Room for Recovery

What happens when things go wrong? How do you recover? We'll cover this more extensively in chapter 14, but here are three common snags:

- Your mind drifts and you lose your train of thought.
- You don't understand what they're saying.
- You're bored.

Your mind drifts.

In the middle of a conversation, you suddenly realize that the other person has stopped talking and is obviously waiting for you to respond. It could be because you let yourself get distracted. But it might be because you were really interested in something they said, and your mind took a little side trip to process the information. You might be thinking about how it applies to you, or some situation you have coming up soon, or something that happened recently.

Once you recognize that you've drifted, don't panic. You probably heard their last few words, so you could pick up on them and simply make a comment about them. But it's easiest to be honest and let them know what happened: "I'm sorry—I missed the last thing you said because I was still thinking about what you said just before that. Can I go back there and ask a question about it?" It's genuine and shows you were actually listening *so* carefully that your mind wasn't ready to move forward yet.

You don't understand what they're saying.

No one wants to appear ignorant, so we have a tendency to pretend we understand when we actually don't. But there's no harm in stopping to ask for clarification.

Author and speaker Kathy Collard Miller has modeled this for me many times. I'll say something to make a point or make what I meant to be a humorous remark. She smiles and says, "I'm not quite with you. Help me understand." The first few times she did that, I remember thinking how refreshing it was. I wished I could be comfortable enough to do that. But I realized that it displayed a level of confidence in herself to have the security to admit she didn't know everything. In effect she was saying, "I really want to understand you and need help to make sure that happens." I also realized that it wasn't an advanced technique that I would have to learn; I simply had to do it.

You're bored.

We try to take good care of the plants in our yard. But no matter what we do, occasionally something just withers and dies. Some people say they have a "brown thumb," meaning that anything they touch in a garden dies. But even if I were an expert gardener, some plants just aren't going to survive. It doesn't say anything about me; it says something about the plant.

No matter how skillful I am at communication, I can't be responsible for both sides of a conversation. I can take care of my side, but I can't force anything to happen on your side. If a conversation isn't working, I have two options:

1. I can explore to discover a person's expertise or passion. People usually talk a lot more freely about the things they're passionate about.
2. If that doesn't work, I can graciously end the conversation and move on.

Homework for Hearing

Pay close attention to the next few conversations you're around. These could be your own conversations or simply watching the interaction between others. Focus on what is being said but also observe the nonverbal signals that are taking place. Notice what people do that makes the other feel connected and what barriers get in the way.

Preparing for a television interview last year, I watched the show a few times to observe the interaction between the hosts and the guests. Some seemed to connect immediately, while others didn't make the connection. I tried to identify what the difference was, and it was all nonverbal. The ones who didn't connect sat back on the couch, didn't have good eye contact with the hosts, and just presented their information. The ones who connected sat forward on the couch and engaged in a focused, personal conversation with the hosts. They seemed unaware of the camera or the surroundings in the studio, blocking out everything except the fact that they were having an intimate conversation.

I asked the hosts what they thought made the best interviews, and it was exactly that. The guests simply had a conversation with them while a few million people watched.

Try just watching for the next few weeks. Be keenly aware of whether or not a conversation is working and carefully observe what is happening on both sides. Then begin practicing those things yourself. The key is to be genuine. If you try to fake your body language, most people will read through it. Learn to genuinely care about the other person and what's important to them. The more real that is, the more your verbal and nonverbal signals will match. The other person will feel listened to, and you'll make the connection you intended.

11

Channeling Stress

Do you ever have any of these symptoms during a conversation?

- The palms of your hands sweat.
- You perspire more than usual.
- Your stomach starts churning.
- Your mouth goes dry, and it's hard to speak.
- Your mind goes blank, and you lose your train of thought.
- Your hands get cold or clammy.
- Your voice shakes.
- Your hands tremble.

If so, you're not alone. In high-stakes, stressful conversations, those nervous symptoms are common. In a group setting we might look around the room, feeling as if we're the only one experiencing these symptoms. We watch other people who appear to be poised and self-confident and wish we could be as calm. No matter how hard we try to appear controlled, these symptoms sneak up on us. It's as if they're announcing our nervousness to the world.

The truth is that everyone feels stress. The more challenging something is the more stress you'll feel. Many top athletes and entertainers talk about the stress they feel before a major event, some becoming physically sick before a major performance. It's normal, it's common, and it can be a positive force for a sharp performance—depending on what you do with it.

Characteristics of Stress

When we experience the negative impact of stress, we wish we could just do away with it. It's hard enough just holding a conversation with some people; it's even worse when our body gives off signals we can't control but which seem obvious to others.

But eliminating all stress would make the situation worse. Without stress, we wouldn't have the creative tension that keeps us focused, using the best tools and skills we've developed to meet the challenge. Everything we do that's worthwhile takes energy. The right amount of stress channels that energy. Too little energy is like a flashlight with low batteries; the light shines, but there isn't enough power to see where we're going.

A violin string needs a certain amount of tension to play in tune. Too little and the string produces no sound; too much and the string breaks. Fear of making conversation isn't something to be eliminated. When used correctly, stress can actually become the fuel for creative interaction.

In a social setting, stress often comes from entering unknown conversational territory. You join a group of people where everyone seems to know each other, and you're the only one who feels out of place. When you're focused on your own performance, you're setting yourself up for greater stress than necessary. You'll feel less stress if you move your focus outward, using the exploring tools that you've collected.

What do we get stressed about in a social situation?

- We're afraid we'll end up alone, with no one to talk to.
- We're afraid we'll be talking with someone and run out of things to say.
- We want to be clever, but we're afraid everyone will think we're boring.
- We're worried about the impression we're making.
- We're worried about saying the wrong thing and being embarrassed.

The list could go on and on. We tend to look at these situations as negative, since they're usually associated with painful interactions. But the stress of those situations holds the energy that, when harnessed, can make our conversations effective and fulfilling.

The most valuable books and resources about handling stress are tools for stress *management*, not stress *elimination*. We don't want to totally get rid of stress. We need to learn how to use it to our advantage.

Stress is like gasoline. When a spark hits the fumes, it explodes. If that occurs in your living room, it's devastating. If it occurs in the engine of your car, it gets you where you're going. The gasoline isn't good or bad; the application is what makes the difference.

When stress is controlled it becomes a powerful tool to use in conversations. The key is to recognize the presence of stress, realize that it's a normal emotion, and harness its power through our perception of it. As Shakespeare said, "Nothing is good or bad, but thinking makes it so."

Hans Selye was one of the early researchers in the field of stress. He studied what stress is, what it does, and how it can be controlled. He suggested that there are two primary types of stress: *distress* and *eustress*. Distress is the bad kind of stress that paralyzes us and keeps us from taking action. Eustress is the good stress that moves us forward when we tap into its energy.[9]

The things that take place are called *stressors*—sources of stress. Interestingly, the stressors are almost always neutral. It's what we tell ourselves about the stressor that determines our response to it.

When our kids were teenagers, we often agreed on what time they would come home from an event. A few times, they didn't make it home by that time. That led to a progressive series of thoughts:

- First, we noticed that they were late.
- After a few minutes, we were thinking that they were pushing the rules, and we'd have to talk about it when they got home.
- As time passed, we began to be irritated.
- As more time passed, irritation turned to concern.
- Then we started to worry.
- If enough time passed, we began to panic, imagining the worst.

The later it got, the worse our stress became. But when the door opened a few minutes or hours later, the panic immediately disappeared. (Of course, a new type of stress took over, based on their excuses.)

The simple fact was that they were late. Our stress came from our interpretation of that event.

When we believe the worst-case scenario, it's hard to convince ourselves to just "stop worrying." In that case we need to analyze our perspective to determine what's real and what's not. If we can change the way we think, we can change the way we feel.

How to Make Stress Work for Us

Someone has said that stress is like having butterflies in your stomach. The key isn't to get rid of the butterflies; it's getting them to fly in formation.

How do we do that? First, we need to analyze what we tell ourselves. Second, we need to take specific actions to channel the stress.

Analyzing Our Thoughts

It's important to recognize what we're telling ourselves. When we feel stress about a conversation, one of three things might be happening:

1. We blame others for the things that happen instead of blaming our interpretation of the events.

When William Glasser wrote the book *Reality Therapy*, he agreed that we have been greatly influenced by our past.

The way we were raised, the environment that surrounded us, and the choices of other people have been factors that shape who we are today. But he suggests that even though we're partially a product of the past, we can make new choices about the future. If we choose to stay the way we are, it's no longer the fault of the people in our past; it's our choice.[10]

In a conversation, it's important to recognize our ability to do things differently than we've done before. For example, in the past, we might have assumed that what other people say or how they act is the cause of conversational breakdown. In reality, it's our interpretation of what they do or say that impacts us the most. It might be true that the other person is making the biggest contribution to ineffective conversation. But blaming them for the breakdown is a reaction on our part that can be just as ineffective.

2. We assume the outcome will be the worst possible scenario.

Before a conversation begins, some people assume that it will be awkward and uncomfortable. They picture themselves being embarrassed when the conversation falters and having the person reject them and walk away. Then they conclude that it would reinforce their poor conversational skills, which they interpret as a personality fault, which makes them assume they'll never be able to make good conversation. The final conclusion is that the situation is hopeless, they'll never be able to make new friends, and their life will be perpetually mediocre.

This is an extreme example but not that far off from what often happens. That's why it's important to catch these downward-spiraling thoughts and put them in a bigger perspective. It's possible that a conversation won't go successfully. But we don't want to assume that will happen. In fact, it's just as likely that a conversation will go well. If we kept track accurately, uncomfortable conversations are a tiny percentage compared to the successful ones. We just remember the negative ones more because they were painful.

Chuck Swindoll is well known for saying that attitude is everything. If a conversation doesn't go well, our attitude will determine how we handle it. We don't carry full responsibility for the success or failure of a conversation. There are at least two people sharing in the outcome. A truth-centered attitude recognizes that fact and doesn't put the total weight of the failure on one's own shoulders.

3. We assume our past has to be the predictor of our future.

Building our future on past performance is common. If I've always been told I'm shy, I'll project that into the future. If something embarrassing happens in a conversation, I assume that every conversation could be embarrassing.

But it's unfair to project one failure onto your whole future. Always speak truth to yourself. Instead of saying, "I'm a failure," replace it with accurate information: "That conversation didn't go quite the way I hoped it would." Instead of saying, "I'm afraid they'll reject me, and I couldn't handle that," say, "If I don't get the response I'd like, it says more about the other person than about me. It might be a little embarrassing, but I'll be OK. I'll move forward."

Channeling Our Stress

Typically, we see stress as a bad thing. But when properly channeled, stress provides the fuel to make a conversation work. When you feel the symptoms of stress, think of it as driving into a gas station. You're filling your tank with something powerful that enables your car to move forward.

Once you've filled your tank (recognized the presence of stress), take practical steps to make sure the power of that fuel is harnessed.

During a conversation:

- Focus on what the other person is saying instead of how you're feeling. This takes practice, but you'll find freedom when you're not worried about your performance.

- Realize that it might take awhile to get a conversation "working." It's kind of like a slow dance with a stranger; you need time to adjust to their style.

- Be prepared. Know your tools for exploring and how to use them.

- Don't take all the credit or blame for the success or failure of a conversation. It takes at least two people to make a conversation work; you're not totally responsible for what happens.

During a group event:

- Start small. In a social situation, try to find someone who looks friendly and approachable or someone you know. You might observe another person who is like you in some way, such as the way they dress or the fact that they're the only other person at the buffet table trying the liver pâté. Practice your conversational skills with that person. It will give you more confidence to talk to someone else, or the other person might lead you to someone else. (Plus, you won't have to initiate as many conversations as the event progresses.)

- Review your "performance" after the "game"—but *only once.* Sports teams study the films of last week's game to see where they can improve for the next game. That's a powerful way to improve your skills. There is real value in thinking through what you did well and what you could learn from.

- Don't compare your performance with that of other people in the room. If you do, you'll probably pick the best conversationalist for comparison, and you'll feel inferior. On the other hand, if you pick the wallflowers, you'll falsely exaggerate your performance. Compare your performance with your own standards—what you've done before and how you want to be in the future.

When you experience symptoms of stress, take action to deal directly with them:

- *Sweaty palms*—Wash your hands frequently. Each time it happens, excuse yourself and do it again. You might also keep a napkin handy. If your symptoms are severe, you may want to contact your physician.

- *Perspiration*—Be sure to use an antiperspirant. Keep a handkerchief or napkin in your pocket to "touch up" your brow if perspiration shows. Excuse yourself if you need to freshen up in the restroom.

- *Upset stomach*—Keep an antacid handy. Make sure you don't have an empty stomach, which can exaggerate the upset feeling. If food is part of the event, be careful to avoid foods you're not used to. Don't let your nervousness cause you to overeat.

- *Cotton mouth*—Drink water throughout the day before attending. Keep some water handy to sip during conversations to minimize the effects of dryness. Just don't overdo it. It's one thing to excuse yourself to use the restroom to escape a boring conversation; it's quite another to have to leave a stimulating conversation because of a biological need.

- *Blank mind*—Before the event, choose some basic topics you could discuss and jot them down on note cards. Try to memorize those topics but have the note cards available. You can glance at them between conversations for a quick review. If you still can't think of where to take a conversation next, end it graciously and warmly. Then check your notes before initiating another conversation.

- *Cold hands*—This is more uncomfortable for you than for the person who shakes your hand. People recognize that different people have different internal temperatures, and their hands simply reflect that. Try not to keep your hands in your pockets during a conversation but do so during your breaks. Replace iced beverages with hot ones if possible, so you can warm your hands on the container.

- *Shaky voice*—Try speaking more slowly and deliberately. Breathe deeply while the other person is speaking; this tends to relax the muscles, including those that help you form speech.

- *Trembling hands*—Most people won't notice this during a conversation unless you're holding a paper or a cup that accentuates the movement. In this case, try not to hold anything while you're talking.

In most of these cases, breathing exercises will minimize the impact of the stress symptoms. Close your eyes and take five slow, deep breaths through your nose, then breathe out in a controlled manner through your mouth. This forces you to relax and focus on the process, which automatically takes your mind off the symptoms you feel. It also increases the amount of oxygen you take in, which provides fuel for your entire body to function properly.

Making the Most of Stress

Stress is a powerful tool for making effective conversation. When we feel stress, it should signal us that something worthwhile is happening. That should trigger us to channel it instead of being paralyzed by it.

First, we can practice *mental* control over the stress. The methods discussed in this chapter focus on evaluating situations accurately and truthfully rather than interpreting situations incorrectly. We can visualize the conversation going well. When it does, we should allow ourselves to enjoy the positive feeling that accompanies it. When it doesn't go well, it's uncomfortable. We need to be realistic about what happened, analyzing what we could do differently next time. But then it's time to let it go instead of repeatedly reviewing the things that went wrong.

For example, assume you have an upcoming conversation with an important person. Some people visualize the negative and it becomes a self-fulfilling prophecy. When you recognize self-defeating thoughts, stop and ask what's true about the situation. Then you can build the right picture.

From everything we've discussed in this book, we know that people usually want to connect with other people. Visualize that. Picture yourself approaching the person you're meeting. Think about how you'll introduce yourself and imagine the conversation going well. Fix that solidly in your mind. Now you're ready for your meeting. In most cases, you'll find your positive mental image to be closer to the reality of what happens.

What if the actual conversation doesn't go as well as you hoped? Take a few moments to think through what happened. Ask yourself, "If I were in that situation again, what could I have said differently? What would have been a better response to their question?" Now that you've gained some benefit from rehearsing it again in your mind, mentally walk away from it. You're done. Once you've given yourself a quick debrief, move on to the next conversation. Don't allow yourself to get stuck in past conversations that you can't change.

Second, we can practice *physical* control over the stress. Instead of assuming that we can't change, we can practice the simple techniques discussed earlier. Many stress symptoms are best handled with breathing techniques, exercises, and the practical suggestions reviewed earlier. It's not always something that needs a psychological solution. If I discover spinach between my teeth after a conversation, I don't need better conversational skills; I just need floss.

Third, we need to practice *often* to learn to manage the stress. When we recognize the value of harnessing that fuel, we'll look forward to every opportunity to practice. The more we practice, the easier it gets. We'll never eliminate stress, nor do we want to. But we can make it one of our greatest allies in making conversation.

12

Developing Curiosity

A curious person is usually a good conversationalist. Since they're curious, they like to investigate everything going on around them. That provides them with more potential topics to talk about. It doesn't mean that they're an expert on every topic. But conversation becomes easier when we know "a little about a lot" and "a lot about a little."

It's kind of like going into a well-stocked local hardware store. They typically don't have huge quantities of anything, but they always seem to have a few of the exact thing you need. That's OK, since you don't need to buy a lot of one thing.

Imagine a store that only sold nails. That would be great if you needed nails, but you'd be out of luck if you needed plywood. You could have a great conversation with the store owner about nails but nothing else. You wouldn't need to visit that store very often.

The more topics we have to draw from our mental "shelves," the easier it is to start a conversation. We don't have to be an expert in everything. But knowing a little about a lot goes a long way in providing ingredients for conversation. In this chapter, we'll learn why it's valuable to nurture your spirit of curiosity and how to spark that desire if it's not naturally there.

Where Does Curiosity Come From?

In seminars, I often draw a black dot on a flip chart with a marker. When I ask a group of adults what it is, they always say it's a black dot. But if I show the same thing to a group of children, nobody ever says it's a dot. Typical responses will include:

- "It's a hole in the ground."
- "It's a squashed bug."
- "It's the top of a telephone pole."
- "It's a drop of ink."
- "It's a ball."

Kids are naturally curious. If you've spent any time around four-year-olds, you know how many times they can ask "Why?" Because of that curiosity, they naturally explore the world around them. Most of that begins with play, using blocks, imagination, words, and various objects. Their experience grows in complexity, but they find pleasure in mastering new ideas. Since they enjoy it, they repeat the activity. No one forces them; they just repeat it for the sheer pleasure. That repetition leads to mastery, which leads to a sense of accomplishment and confidence. When they feel confident, they want to keep exploring their world. The cycle begins and ends with curiosity.

As adults, there's a real danger in competence. When we're good at something, we tend to lose our curiosity. After all, what we're doing is working well, so we may not feel a strong drive to challenge the process or do it differently. This lack of curiosity is made worse by the daily challenges of our job and things that are constantly changing in a work or home environment. There's so much going on, we look for something that provides routine and stability. That often takes the form of doing what we know how to do well.

When we painted our house a couple of years ago, we did it ourselves. It took awhile, but we were pleased with the results. What amazed us, though, was the reaction we got from people. They were simply in awe that we could do the work ourselves instead of calling a professional. One person said, "I wouldn't know where to start if I wanted to paint my house."

There's also a danger in complexity. We recently bought a couple of new appliances for our kitchen. The labels include a strict warning that any repair work needs to be done by a qualified technician, implying that it's beyond the abilities of the owners to try to fix it themselves. It used to be that people would try to repair something first and call a repair shop as a last resort. Today that tends to be reversed; we call for help before investigating.

Curiosity May Have Killed the Cat, but It's a Tonic for Successful Conversation

Being good at making conversation will be a process. We won't become experts overnight. But a curious mind becomes fertile ground for conversations to grow and bear fruit.

The more curious we are, the more things we have to talk about. There are a lot of things we can do to increase our curiosity. Notice how different personality types (based on the Myers-Briggs Type Indicator) might increase their curiosity:

- *Intuitive Feelers* are reflective, so curiosity comes pretty naturally to them. They use imagination and imagery to look at things in new ways. They might use journaling as a way to capture and organize observations and will focus on how those inputs made them feel. If they spend a day at Disneyland, they'll take their time walking through the park, noticing the details of design. At the end of their visit, they'll remember the different parts of their day based on how each event made them feel.

- *Intuitive Thinkers* are analytical, so they'll be asking detailed questions about the things they observe: who, what, when, how, where, and why. They make sure they have all the facts and then spend time thinking of the implications and applications for everyday life. A day at Disneyland will find them studying the number of people present, how long the lines are, and how those long lines are affecting them. They'll remember what they encountered based on the meaning they found in each event.

- *Sensory Judges* like concrete ideas rather than abstract concepts. They use their senses of sight, sound, and touch to observe the world and will think through the logical implications. They're more interested in the details than the application. At the end of a Disneyland trip, they can tell you all the facts they learned throughout the day. They know how long it took to wait for each ride, what the problems were with pedestrian traffic patterns, and how to fix each of those problems.

- *Sensory Perceivers* are good at multitasking and learn by doing. They will glean insights from participating in activities. At Disneyland, they're too busy enjoying the day to analyze what's happening. If they remember details of the day, it's because they're telling stories about what they were doing throughout the experience.[11]

Nurturing curiosity is similar to photography. I once heard a photographer from *Arizona Highways* magazine speak, and he was asked what makes his photos so unique. He said that he would look at the same thing other people were seeing but would try to figure out what it would look like from a different perspective: from higher, or lower, or under the light of the setting or rising sun, or on a cloudy day. He used his curiosity to think of different ways to perceive it, which produced a photograph that stood apart in quality. People would be amazed at the result because it forced them to look at something they had already seen but from a different perspective.

In its simplest form, curiosity is simply looking at something common from a different angle.

In a practical sense, it's not hard to nurture your curiosity. If you've let yours get a little rusty, a few practical exercises can get it back into shape again:

- Skim the newspaper each day. Read the articles you find interesting but also glance through a few that stretch you a bit. Write down any key items you observe and ask yourself the standard journalism questions: who, what, when, where, how, and why. Read between the lines and look for reasons and motives. That means you'll be reading the same information as others do but seeing something else.

- Look for things around you that you don't normally notice. Take a walk along a busy city street and listen for sounds that aren't man-made. Even when you're close to traffic, it's possible to hear a bird sing.

- While walking down a street, try to imagine what's going on in the minds of the people you pass. Watch their facial expressions; try to imagine what their day has been like and where they're headed.

- As you make discoveries, write down what you find. From those observations, develop a list of questions you don't know the answer to. The next time you're in a conversation with someone, bring up a few of those questions to find their perspective.

- When you're watching television, ask the journalism questions (who, what, where, when, how, and why) about the shows. Picture the writers working together to develop a script for the show. Think through a different ending for a drama you've seen.

- Be like a little kid and ask "Why?" repeatedly. Don't use that exact word out loud, over and over in a conversation, but let the question guide your exploration and discussion. It's a great tool for developing curiosity and getting the information you want.

- Explore the uncharted territory of each conversation. Consciously work to discover things you didn't know when you started.

There are three primary times when curiosity will come in handy: before a conversation, during a conversation, and after a conversation. Develop a sense of curiosity, and you'll be able to hold your own in those times. Remember—you're exploring, and there's a lot of hidden treasure. Your job is to find it. But if it doesn't occur to you that the treasure even exists, you'll never look for it—or find it.

Here's the key to success in conversations: Assume that each person you talk to knows something you don't that's interesting. Make it your goal to find out what it is. Explore their responses to get under the surface. You don't have to have a list of topics in mind; the other person is where you'll find those topics. If you're genuinely curious to find out the details of their interests, you'll have a much easier time making conversation.

13

Using Questions Effectively

As I walked into the choir rehearsal, my friend Thom was sitting just inside the door. "How are you?" he asked. "Fine," I replied.

"Thirty-seven."

"Thirty-seven?" I said. "What about thirty-seven?"

Thom said, "Just watch." Soon the next person entered the room. "Hi," Thom said. "How are you?"

"Fine," the man replied.

"Thirty-eight." Thom had asked the same question of thirty-eight people and gotten the same response. It's one of those questions we all use to break the ice in a conversation, not really expecting a detailed response.

Most people assume that the best way to make conversation is to ask a lot of questions. When used properly, good questions can move a conversation forward, giving you an endless supply of material to explore in communication with someone. Using weak questions is like planting a tree in your backyard but using a teaspoon to dig the hole. Those types of questions can leave both people frustrated and grind the conversation to a halt. That's why it's critical to use the strongest questions possible for any given situation.

Most people ask questions from their own background and experience. They listen to what the other person says through their own frame of reference, interpreting their conversation through their own filters. It's important to remember that questions are tools for exploring. We use them to find new information in a conversation that wasn't there when the encounter started. A person who is good at making conversation will form their questions from the listener's perspective, not simply their own experience.

Types of Questions

Questions can take a lot of different forms. But for our purposes, we'll divide them into two categories: *closed-ended questions* and *open-ended questions*.

Closed-ended questions are those that can be answered with one or two words, primarily "yes" or "no." Usually they are fairly weak tools, ineffective for making good conversation. They do have their place but usually just at the beginning of a conversation to get things started.

I don't mean that closed-ended questions are bad; they're just limited in what they can accomplish. They're good when you're looking for basic information from someone rather than opinion or perspective. If you want to know where someone works, what time it is, or the location of the restroom, a closed-ended question is appropriate: "Where do you work?" In the early stages of a conversation, closed-ended questions can be a good starting point for discovering new areas to explore.

It's like opening a vault where you know there is treasure inside. The closed-ended questions open the vault. But once you're inside, you want to switch to open-ended questions to mine the treasure.

Open-ended questions are powerful tools for exploring new territory in your attempt to find common ground. They make it difficult to respond with single-word answers and encourage the person to expand their thoughts. Used wisely, they have a myriad of benefits:

- They make it easier for you in the conversation, because you get the other person talking about themselves and their opinions. That person does all the work—you just steer the conversation and listen!

- They make the other person feel safe with you. Open-ended questions allow the person to decide how much or how little they are comfortable sharing. That gives them the feeling that they're the ones in control of the conversation, when you're actually the one steering the flow.

- When people hear a long list of closed-ended questions which require only quick responses, they feel like they're being interrogated. They usually feel intimidated by that style, and communication is hindered. Open-ended questions keep that from happening, since it takes longer for them to answer.

- Good open-ended questions build trust. The other person feels like you genuinely care about them, because you're interested in what they have to say. They sense that you listened carefully enough to craft appropriate questions, and you're paying attention to their responses. When people feel that you genuinely care, strong relationships are built.

- When you ask open-ended questions, you don't have to pretend you know everything. Your curiosity is what enables you to ask these questions. Open-ended questions take the pressure off, allowing you to relax and enjoy the exchange. You get to choose the direction of the conversation when you use open-ended questions.

Using open-ended questions is like driving a car. In reality, the engine does all the work; you just steer. Closed-ended questions are like pushing the car and trying to steer through the window. It's possible, but it's a lot of work and you won't go very fast. If you do, you'll probably run into something.

Using Questions Effectively

Open-ended questions can build and maintain momentum during a conversation. For example, someone introduces you to a friend and tells you they spent time in the Middle East. You might start with open-ended questions:

"What took you to the Middle East?"

If they respond briefly ("the military"), you might use a couple of closed-ended questions to get more information and then move back to open-ended ones.

1. "Which branch of the military?" (closed-ended)
2. "What made you choose the navy?" (open-ended)

3. "I think of Iraq as a desert. What does the navy do in the desert?" (open-ended)
4. "What was your time like there?" (open-ended)
5. "What was a typical day like for you?" (open-ended)

Notice that the open-ended questions give the listener the opportunity to expand on the topic. Closed-ended questions require a short answer and don't encourage the person to keep talking:

1. Instead of "Was it hot there?" (closed) ask, "What was the weather like while you were there?" (open)
2. Instead of "Are you planning to go back?" (closed) ask, "What are the things you experienced that would take you back someday?" (open)
3. Instead of "Did you miss your family?" (closed) ask, "What was it like being away from your family for so long?" (open)

As they're responding, listen carefully for new information they offer. Focusing on new information provides options for forming your next question. Think of yourself as a news reporter, asking the six questions we discussed earlier that are part of every story: *who, what, when, where, how,* and *why.* Turn those six basic questions into open-ended exploring tools and you'll learn more than you expected about most topics.

If you're genuinely interested in what they're saying, encourage them. A simple statement like, "Interesting—tell me more" gives them the incentive to keep talking. Other encouraging responses could include:

1. "I'm not sure I would have handled the situation as well as you did. How did it make you feel?"

2. "What an incredible experience. How has it impacted you since it happened?"

3. "This is exactly the information I was looking for. What else can you tell me?"

The same applies to everyday conversations with family members and friends. Instead of asking, "How was your day?" simply say, "Tell me about your day." A simple change in wording can make the difference in the quality and length of the response you receive.

Early in any conversation in a large gathering, ask open-ended questions like, "What brings you here?" "What's your connection with this group?" "How do you know the host?" As you learn about their experience, background, and expertise, pick up on anything that you share in common and pursue it. Maybe you grew up in the same state, or had some experience with their company, or had the same major in college. The longer the conversation goes, the more common ground you'll discover about each other.

Tips for Talking

The basic skill of asking questions is pretty straightforward. But in an actual conversation, things can go wrong unexpectedly. The next chapter will focus on handling tough conversations. But when you're asking questions, watch what's happening. If "red flags" catch your attention, be prepared to adapt some of the following strategies to keep from losing control:

- Don't start a conversation with hard questions or deep questions. You have to build trust first. As you practice the techniques in this book over time, you're going to feel more comfortable starting conversations. You might be eager to demonstrate those new conversational skills and imply that you're too "deep" for small talk. But the listener might be taken aback by questions that go too deep too soon and might feel uncomfortable. Take time to build trust first, and then let the conversation get deeper naturally over time.

- When you're using open-ended questions, make sure they're specific enough to focus the conversation. If you ask a question like, "So, what do you think about politics?" you'll probably get a limited response. The listener feels overwhelmed at how much they could say, so they don't even bother to answer. Keeping your questions focused gives the listener some boundaries to work with, which makes them more comfortable in responding.

- Only ask questions you really want answers to. They'll sense if you really don't care, and they'll realize you're just using the questions as a gimmick. The other risk is that they'll take your simple question and give you more information than you ever wanted.

- Plan your questions in advance. For example, I have a conference call next week with the CEO of a company I'll be working with soon. I've never met him, so I went onto his company website and read his biographical information. I saw several points of common ground that I could speak about, so I've planned questions that relate to his background and interests. I also have some specific information I need to obtain from him, so I'll make sure my questions draw out the appropriate answers.

- It's OK to write out your questions. To some people it feels artificial. They assume that if we really cared we would just remember without prompting. But there's a lot going on in our minds, and organizing it in an easy-to-remember outline demonstrates that you cared enough to take the time to make the biggest impact possible. When I call that CEO, I'll have my list of questions in front of me. That way I can relax and focus on our conversation, feeling free to explore the new information he provides.

- Have a few generic follow-up questions ready. Memorize them so they're available if and when you need them. If you're sitting with a group at a table and the conversation stops, use one or two of them to get things moving again. If you feel that a topic has simply run out of steam, just change gears and ask a question to take the group in a new direction. Start with a couple of closed-ended questions to explore for interest, or bring up something you gleaned from listening to the group earlier.

- Make flash cards with possible topics and questions to ask. It might seem elementary, but schools still use them because they work. Keep them in your car, and review two or three every time you get out of the car. You could also keep them by your phone or in your purse or billfold. Review them when you're waiting on hold or in line. Over time, they'll become part of your memory so you can draw from them when needed.

- Watch out for risky questions. People's lives change over time, so be careful making assumptions if you haven't seen the person for a while. It could be uncomfortable when you ask about their spouse, their job, or their children only to find out that they're divorced, unemployed, and dealing with wayward kids. You don't know if they're going through painful times or not, so be sure you phrase your questions carefully. Say something such as, "The last time we talked, you were struggling with some tough decisions about your job. How did that turn out?" Or, "What's the latest with your son?" This type of questioning is honest, since you're not ignoring the obvious issues you both know about. But it approaches the subject cautiously, being sensitive to any issues that might have come up in their life.

- If you don't understand what someone is saying, ask. We're often afraid that if we ask for clarification they'll think we're not listening. In reality, it does the opposite. Taking the time to gain an accurate understanding will reinforce their perception of you as a good listener. That's because you're listening carefully enough to make sure you get it correct.

- If the conversation stalls, don't assume that the other person is boring. It might just be that you're asking the wrong questions or focusing the conversation more on you than on the other person. Professional salespeople realize that if they're going to be effective in connecting with customers, they have to get the customer to do 70 percent of the talking.

- The key is to make sure you're really interested in their answer, not just in how good your question is. Listen to their answer rather than thinking about what you're going to say when they're finished.

What to Do When You're on the Receiving End

We've been discussing ways to focus the conversation on the other person. That's appropriate, because that's where we need to put our effort to be effective in our part of a conversation. I can't control another person, but I can make choices about what I do.

But conversation is a two-way street. Sometimes the conversation goes well without your interference. The other person is interested in you and begins exploring your experience. You'll recognize when it's happening, because they're using the same techniques you do.

I had coffee with Jim this morning, and he demonstrated an unusual level of skill in balancing a conversation. I asked him questions and explored new areas to discuss. He was comfortable answering and filling me in on the details of his life. But at regular intervals he did the exact same thing to me, asking open-ended questions about things he remembered from a conversation a few months earlier. Both of us got to ask questions, and both of us felt listened to. At the end, we both walked away feeling satisfied about our time together.

So, how do you answer questions when they are aimed your direction?

- Honestly. Mark Twain said that you don't need a good memory if you always tell the truth. People respect candor in a conversation, so make sure you speak with integrity. It's the basis for any effective communication.

- If you're not sure how to answer, ask a clarifying question to "buy time." It will ensure that you have time to think through a thoughtful response. You don't have to hide what you're doing; just be honest and tell them that you need a minute to think about what they've asked so you can give them an accurate perspective.

- Use humor like a scalpel—sparingly and carefully. Never tell jokes, especially with people you've just met. Just keep a lighthearted view of life, and let that come through your conversation.

- If you don't know the answer to something they've asked, be honest and tell them you'll get back with them in a few days. Ask if they prefer a response by phone or by email, and make sure you have their contact information. Then make sure you respond in a timely fashion. People remember when you don't do what you've promised, as well as when you do.

- If you're having trouble reading their response because of little or no facial expression, ask if you've answered their question. You could also say, "Those are my thoughts; what do *you* think?" or "Does that make sense?"

- Tell a story to illustrate your position. Make sure the length of the story fits the depth of the question. When you're telling a good story, there's a danger of adding too much detail and boring the other person.

   For instance, the person you're talking with mentions having a ficus tree in their yard. You've had one and experienced problems with the roots. Telling your story briefly could set up the next topic of discussion: "A ficus tree? Those are beautiful, and we loved the one we had. But we had to cut it down when the roots destroyed our sidewalk. Have you had problems like that?" Notice how you presented your story but kept the emphasis on the other person.

Caring and Sharing

People form relationships with people they like. If you talk to them about the things that matter to them, they'll like you. Think how you've been drawn to someone when they truly listened to you.

You don't have to have as many right answers if you have the right questions. Start with asking the six journalism questions about a topic. You don't have to appear brilliant. Just ask carefully crafted questions, and you can relax.

Don't get discouraged if you don't feel completely comfortable right away. Like anything of value, using appropriate questions takes practice. Pick one question and use it over the next couple of days until you feel comfortable. Then, add other techniques one at a time. As your skill grows, so will your confidence.

Here's a quick summary of how to use questions effectively in any conversation:

1. Ask a close-ended question.
2. Follow up by asking the reporter's open-ended questions: who, what, where, when, how, and why.
3. Listen carefully to the person's response.
4. Repeat.

It's that simple!

14

Handling Tough Conversations

No matter what your skill level, eventually you'll end up in a conversation that becomes uncomfortable. That most often happens when someone has a different personality style than you do, and it's good to be prepared with some basic approaches to use in any situation. You'll know how to respond in those tough conversations and avoid being manipulated.

Sometimes you just sense that a conversation is moving downhill. Knowing how to watch for that downward slide makes it easier to handle, because you can take action before it's too late. But sometimes that nosedive takes place suddenly, when you're not expecting it. Let's look at some of the most common things that go wrong and some possible solutions.

What to Do . . .

When Someone Disagrees with You

If someone comes to your door to sell you a new vacuum cleaner, you won't have a very good chance of selling them yours instead. No matter how good your intentions are, it just won't happen. They're in the "selling" mind-set, which makes it hard to convince them to "buy." So any attempt will be futile.

When someone strongly disagrees with us or attacks us, there's a natural tendency to defend ourselves and fight back. But you don't want to become adversarial, especially in the first few conversations. If they present an objectionable point, it's usually futile to try to change their mind in this conversation. If they've brought the point up this early, they're not in the "buying" mind-set.

Instead, work to understand their position better. They'll be more open to talking with you, and you've gained more information about how they think. It doesn't mean you'll end up agreeing with them. But you're approaching the conversation with a spirit of humility.

Look at the disagreement as a chance to analyze your position by comparing it with another person's views. Humility means accepting the possibility that your position isn't necessarily perfect. If you stay calm, avoid defensiveness, and listen deeply to what they're saying, you'll have a much clearer view of your position as well as theirs.

Look for areas where you do agree. If you realize that some part of your position is wrong or inaccurate, admit it and apologize. If you need time to think before responding, tell them that you're going to do exactly that. It's better to think carefully and email your response than to feel forced into saying something you'll regret.

Possible response: "That's really an interesting way to look at it. I've always believed just the opposite, and you're the first person I've met that feels so strongly about your position. I'd love to hear more about how you reached your perspective."

When Someone Is Rude

There's no place for rude behavior among adults. As one older woman I know says, "They should know better." But sometimes they don't, and it happens anyway. When it does, be careful not to get sucked into their behavior. You don't want to debate someone who doesn't play fair.

You might feel the need to confront them about their rude behavior. That's difficult to do in the middle of the conflict. If it's a colleague or someone you have to interact with on a regular basis, you might want to plan a gentle approach at another time that's appropriate for their temperament. This could be effective for someone you're close to. But with someone you don't know it might be ineffective.

A rude person often isn't sensitive to the impact of their words. If you need to say something, give a calm, measured response such as "Ouch!" or "Did you really mean to come across the way you just did?" If it alerts them to their rude behavior and prompts them to change, you've rescued the conversation by making them aware. If not, just excuse yourself and get away. It's OK to leave a conversation in which you're being verbally abused. Don't get upset, because that puts them in control. Just express your need to end the conversation and walk away. If possible, join another conversation immediately as a way to get back on a positive note quickly.

Possible response: "Well, that was uncomfortable. I'm guessing you didn't mean to phrase that exactly the way you did, right?"

When the Other Person Is Angry

The Bible says, "A gentle answer turns away wrath" (Prov. 15:1). When a person becomes angry or displays strong emotion, they generally become unable to hear logic. If you try to reason with this person, their anger might increase. In this case it's best to use the skills of careful listening described in chapter 10. When you take the time to simply identify with what they're feeling, you've given them exactly what they need to begin working through the emotion. From that point, they might become open to discussing the issue calmly and logically.

Watch your own emotions. Anger is contagious; make sure you don't "catch it."

Possible response: "You feel strongly about this, don't you?"

When Someone Uses Inappropriate Humor

This fits in the same category as being rude. The person thinks they're helping the conversation, but they're actually making it worse. People are uncomfortable, but often no one says anything. Should you?

If it's someone you're close to or have a relationship with, it might be worth talking to them about it—usually at a later time in a neutral environment. If it's someone you don't know, you could make a carefully worded response that doesn't put them down but lets them know that they said something inappropriate.

If it continues you could just walk away, which indicates the same thing. Don't feel as if you need to fix the other person's behavior. It took them a long time to get this way, and you won't fix it with a single comment. If you really need to converse with them, craft your response and time it carefully. Remember, your goal is to help them see what they're doing—not to fix them. If your response comes across as criticism, it won't change anything.

> Possible response: "OK, that was awkward. I guess it's time to move to another topic" (or another conversation).

When a Person Becomes Critical

When someone criticizes you, it feels like they're throwing knives at you. What's the best way to handle that?

- Don't ignore it—you'll get hit.
- Don't pretend it didn't happen—they'll keep throwing.
- Don't excuse their behavior—it doesn't help anybody.
- Don't attack them in return—that's what they're expecting.

Instead, stay calm and explore the source of their criticism. Ask for details so you can accurately evaluate what's being said. There may be parts of the criticism you can agree with. If so, acknowledge it. The easiest thing is to agree with their right to their opinion, even if it's different than yours. Don't spend a lot of energy trying to convince them that they're wrong. When they're convinced that they're right, they really don't welcome input from anyone else at that moment.

This happened to me once when I was hired to teach seminars for a company. One of the current trainers was unhappy about my addition to the geographical area where he worked.

He started criticizing me inside the company before he even met me, telling everyone how quickly I would fail and that I would never reach his reputation in local companies. Instead of defending myself, I made a white "surrender" flag with a small dowel and a piece of white cloth. I wrote a message on the flag, acknowledging that I knew he was well-known in the area and that he had a reputation for doing the best seminars in the country (which was true). I wrote that I wanted to cooperate instead of compete and looked forward to partnering with him in the territory. I sent it in a mailing tube, and I received a call a few days later apologizing for his preconceptions. This was a way of honestly dealing with criticism in a way that lessened it instead of escalating the conflict.

> Possible response: "I really want to understand where you're coming from and why you feel so strongly. Can you fill me in on the specific areas where you have concern about my position?"

When People Constantly Complain

Some people have developed the habit of being pessimistic. They've been that way for so long that they don't just see the glass as "half-empty"—they complain about the size of the glass.

You won't be able to change these people in a single conversation. It's taken them a lifetime of experiences to get that way, so it'll take time to reverse it. In this situation, it's probably best to find a time when you can sit down casually in a neutral situation and ask them questions about how their perspective comes across to others and how it damages their relationships. This won't work if you don't genuinely care about them, because they'll sense that you're more concerned about fixing the irritation than about your relationship with them.

> Possible response: "Why don't we grab a cup of coffee next week? I've got some things I'd like to bounce around with you."

When People Pressure You

Occasionally you'll find someone who is committed to changing *your* behavior. Maybe they think you'd be happier if you joined a certain group, or changed your hairstyle, or bought a pet. Trying to reason with them is usually futile, because they've already made up their mind. Instead, be simple and gracious with your response. Say something such as, "No thanks, I don't want to do that." If they keep pressuring you, don't debate their points. Just repeat that same phrase over and over, no matter what arguments they make. It's a point they really can't refute, and eventually they'll quit asking when they know you're not going to change your answer.

> Possible response: "No thanks, I'm not going to participate."

When a Person Talks Too Much

Some people talk incessantly, and you may find it hard to get a word in edgewise. After a while, it becomes a painful effort. So either excuse yourself (they probably won't notice, because they're busy talking) or grab something they've said and ask a new question to take them in a new direction. If this doesn't work after a few times, leave. Don't waste your energy.

Possible response: "That's a great point you're making. In fact, it reminds me of . . ."

When Someone Constantly Interrupts

An occasional interruption is forgivable. But what should you do when it happens repeatedly, where someone interrupts you in the middle of what you're saying and takes the conversation a whole different direction?

Put up your hand and say, "Hang on—let me finish my thought before we change topics." If it keeps happening, they're not listening, and they're more interested in a monologue than in a conversation. This may be a signal to begin wrapping up the conversation and moving on. Remember the basic difference between a monologue and a dialogue. A monologue only takes one person. Don't feel bad leaving a monologue; you're not needed to make it successful.

If someone walks up and interrupts your current conversation, concentrate and stay focused on your conversation. Acknowledge the newcomer but set boundaries. They shouldn't be able to conversationally steal you away from the other person any more than they should be able to walk up and take food off your plate.

Possible response: "Just a second—if I don't finish this thought, it'll disappear into thin air."

What's My Responsibility?

You probably noticed that many of the situations listed have a common solution: walking away. That doesn't mean you're just escaping every situation that is uncomfortable. It means you're making choices about what happens in your conversation. There's no "rule" that says we have to rescue every conversation that gets strained, especially if we're not the one who messed it up. Fortunately, tough conversations are the exception. When things begin to get rough, analyze what's happening and determine whether the wisest choice is to try to repair it or end it. Walking away is a valid choice when you've determined that continuing wouldn't be in your best interest.

Stress-Free Connections

The ideas listed in this chapter aren't gimmicks to manipulate other people and their behavior. The key to making them work is to be honestly and genuinely interested in the other person. We're not trying to learn techniques for "winning" a conversation when it gets tough; we're genuinely trying to make the conversation work for both parties. Any ulterior motives will interfere with effective communication.

There are no guarantees of success, no matter what you try. You can't control other people's choices; you can only control your own. If someone in a tense situation isn't responding to your attempts to deal graciously and effectively with the issues, you don't have to stay in that conversation. Excuse yourself graciously and walk away. Learn from the encounter, and use it as preparation for the next one.

In a gym locker room recently, a controversial news story was on the television. One man reacted by saying, "What a jerk!" He then proceeded to angrily comment on the story and offer his strong opinions of what was being reported. It caught me so off guard that I didn't know what to say, if anything. I walked away wondering how I could have responded. Then I realized that the other person wasn't looking for my opinion; he just wanted to state his.

Looking back, I realized that it was OK that I didn't respond. But I also realized that it would have been valuable to have a few generic responses ready for situations like that, just in case I wanted to say something. "Interesting observation," I could have said. "What makes you say that?" I wouldn't have to agree or disagree. I could just listen. When there was nothing else to say, I could end the conversation graciously and leave.

Handling tough conversations is more of an art form than a science. There's no perfect way to handle those times. But genuinely caring and being prepared are the best tools to feel comfortable and take control when those conversations take place.

15

Attitude Is Everything

Sheila and Tom were driving to a friend's wedding together. They encountered heavy traffic, and Tom became more and more agitated. Sheila tried to convince him to calm down, but that made matters worse. It really wasn't anyone's fault; they were just stuck in traffic. She couldn't understand why he was so upset; he couldn't understand how she could remain so calm.

They were both in the same situation. But one of them was upset; the other one wasn't. What made the difference? It all comes down to *attitude*.

It's true that attitude is important. Different people have different responses to the same situation. The situation may be neutral, but their attitude and mind-set determine how they feel about it.

That's true in making conversation as well. The right attitude in approaching a conversation can make up for techniques that are less than perfect. We might be concerned about whether we're saying the right thing in the right way and how the other person is responding. But if our attitude is one of genuine caring and understanding, there is a lot more room for less-than-perfect techniques.

There are two primary areas of attitude to consider:

- How we feel about *others*
- How we feel about *ourselves*

Monitor Your Attitude about Others

"Can you teach people to care about another person?" That was my question to Jeremy over coffee. He's always been a good sounding board for ideas, and I wanted his input. The question came from research I had been doing for this chapter. Most of what I found focused on how to *appear* to care—what we say, how we say it, and how to subtly manipulate a conversation to make people think we're being genuine. But I found very little about genuine, heartfelt caring.

Jeremy suggested that from his experience, caring isn't something you learn from a book or from someone suggesting that it's a good thing to do. It comes from experiencing it yourself. When you're in a relationship in which someone has genuinely and unconditionally cared about you, it gives you the potential to do the same with someone else. If you haven't experienced that type of genuine caring, you won't recognize it enough to give it to others. "You can't take a person somewhere that you haven't gone yourself," he said.

Giving or Taking?

Henry Drummond said, "Half the world is on the wrong scent in the pursuit of happiness. They think it consists in having and getting, and in being served by others. On the contrary, it consists in giving, and in serving others."[12]

That's the message Dale Burke shares in his book *Less Is More Leadership*. "Serving others in humility does not lower one's leadership potential, it actually increases it. Less 'me' in my leadership makes me 'more' of a leader."[13]

Caring can't be faked. If we develop the attitude of serving others and meeting their needs, we'll find success in the various conversations we take part in. It takes the focus off us and puts it on others.

Being interested in others is practical wisdom that provides a foundation for making any relationship work. If I put my energy into getting the other person to meet my needs, it forces them to do the same. It sets up a relationship built on selfishness. But if I focus on meeting the other person's needs above my own and they do the same, we can base the relationship on a spirit of giving rather than taking. That builds long-term trust and powerful relationships.

What if you don't have a good example—someone who has deeply cared for you unconditionally? That doesn't mean your situation is hopeless. It means you'll learn from someone else's example and practice caring with others, watching how they respond.

Notice that the emphasis is on our responsibility, not the other person's behavior. We can't control someone else; we can only influence. My job is to become the right kind of person, focusing on my own integrity and actions. When that happens, other people will tend to respond differently.

There are no guarantees that they'll do their part, but I'm only responsible for my side of the relationship.

Focusing Outward

I once heard a psychologist describe what happened each day as he turned his car into the driveway of his home. He was exhausted from talking with people all day, and he just wanted to go in and unwind. If he were honest, the last thing he wanted to do each evening was help in the kitchen and do sixth-grade homework. It would have been a lot easier to simply tell his family how tired he was and hope they understood. But his wife and eleven-year-old daughter were his real priority. As he turned off his car's engine at the end of the day he told himself aloud, "I'm now getting ready to do the most important work of my entire day." He chose to have the right attitude, and it had a huge impact on those relationships.

No matter what we're feeling, we can do the same thing. If we have an attitude of entitlement, feeling that we deserve our "comfort zone," we'll experience all of the pain that comes from being focused only on ourselves and our needs. But if we choose an attitude of serving others, we've built a foundation for strong relationships. That type of relationship is what gives us the ability to build strong conversations.

On a trip to Ethiopia several years ago, I was uncertain about communicating with people there since I wasn't familiar with the Amharic language. During the flight, I learned a few useful words and phrases in the Amharic language from my friend Steve, who had been there many times before. The people we would be working with spoke enough English to hold a simple conversation, but I felt it would be a little embarrassing to consider dropping in my elementary phrases in their language. Upon arrival, I found that they appreciated my shaky efforts because they knew I was making an attempt to meet their needs. They chuckled at my pronunciation, but we formed a quick bond because they knew I was reaching out to them.

Not making those kinds of attempts can seem arrogant to them. It's as if we're saying, "I don't need to make things easier for you, and I'm not even going to bother to try. You need to communicate in my language to make things easier for me."

I can't force you to like me, take interest in me, or meet my needs. You are free to choose how you feel and how you act toward me. The more I try to make you do anything, the more frustrated I'll be when you don't cooperate.

The only thing I have control over is my own choices. I can choose what I say to you, how I act toward you, and how I feel about you. I can choose to meet your needs. You can't force me to do that; it's a choice I have to make.

So what *can* I do? I can't control you, but I can influence you. The choices I make will influence the choices you make. If I choose to meet your needs, that will have an influence on the choices you make.

So, what are the basic needs people have? To be *known* and *appreciated*. Being known means that people have taken the time to focus on us, investing their energy in our lives. They recognize that we exist and interact with us on that basis. Being *appreciated* means that they like us and demonstrate that connection.

Monitor Your Attitude about Yourself

The way we think determines who we really are, since our thoughts lead to our attitude. That's why our attitude is so important: it's an accurate description of what's really going on inside. In turn, our attitude determines our actions and choices.

Our *thoughts* lead to our *attitude*, which leads to our *actions*.

We were born with our own unique personality. The key to success isn't to change that uniqueness, it's to learn to accept it and celebrate it. Once we get a clear picture of who we are and our distinct characteristics, we're able to develop that unique design to impact others.

A few chapters ago we discussed the impact of self-talk. We saw that what we believe about ourselves directly impacts our ability to connect with others. If we see ourselves through a negative lens, we'll assume that other people are seeing us that way too (and it will change the way we talk to them). If we see ourselves through a realistic, positive lens, we'll assume that others see us that way as well.

So it's important to see ourselves accurately. What are the positive lenses that will have the greatest impact?

The Lens of Acceptance

Recognize that not every conversation has to be perfect. When we strive for perfection, we'll see ourselves as a failure every time a conversation doesn't go the way we planned. That experience will lessen our view of our abilities and will impact the next conversation that follows, since our lens has gotten cloudy and unrealistic. Like an avalanche, the downward process picks up speed and grows as it progresses.

By contrast, success breeds success. Every time a conversation goes well, it builds our confidence. These successes can provide a growing expectation for success in future interactions.

The Lens of Perspective

It's uncomfortable when someone doesn't connect well with you, but it's critical to keep that in perspective. One negative person's opinion shouldn't be seen as a reliable yardstick for measuring our personal worth.

I've often thought of how difficult it must be for people who hold political office. Take a mayor, for instance. No matter what decision he or she makes, half of the people in town won't like it. It takes a realistic perspective to handle that kind of reaction from people.

When I lead a seminar for one hundred people, the participants are asked to fill out an evaluation form at the end of the day. On a ten-point scale, I might have ninety-nine people who rate the day as a 9 or 10, while one person says it was a 5. My natural tendency is to stew all evening about that 5 and wonder what I could have done differently to get a higher score. But in this case, the majority score is what's really accurate. If one person feels negative about what you've said and ninety-nine feel positive about it, it's not your problem—it's the one person's. But if it's reversed, it's your problem.

If one person tells you you're a horse, ignore it. If ten people tell you you're a horse, it's time to buy a saddle.

The Lens of Positivity

The goal of making conversation is to make connection, not to get the other person to write you into their will.

If you're a quiet person, don't compare yourself with the most outgoing speaker in the room. It's not realistic and is comparing apples and oranges. Anytime you compare yourself with someone else, you're going to see yourself unrealistically. The key is to recognize your uniqueness, accept it, and run with it. When you truly do that, you'll have a positive outlook that comes from within. That, in turn, will attract others.

The Lens of Gratefulness

Everyone seems to be busy, so time is a valuable commodity. When someone spends time talking with you, they're giving you a valuable gift. Recognizing how much it means that they would give you their time will change the way you interact with that person.

Even if they're not the perfect conversational partner, you're receiving something no one else has at that moment: their attention. Enjoy it—don't always be mentally rushing toward the next conversation.

The Lens of Contentment

This is an attitude that comes from inside, when you have a clear acceptance of who you are and what you're about. It's a peaceful recognition that we're not performing for others; we're sharing part of ourselves with another person, and they're doing the same. The result can be a satisfying contact in which both people have given of themselves.

Years ago, J. R. Ewing was a character on *Dallas*, a television program about an oil family in Texas. He was known for his deception and manipulation. In one episode, a friend asked how he could treat people so ruthlessly. He responded, "All you have to do is give up your integrity. If you do that the rest is easy."

Integrity is when the person you are on the outside is the same as the person you are on the inside. Contentment comes when those two are in alignment, because you don't have to put out so much effort pretending you're something you're not.

When Dale Burke became our pastor, his wife was interviewed in front of the congregation. Someone asked her what she could tell us about him that hadn't come out in our interviews with her husband. She said, "The person you see in the pulpit is exactly the same person I see in my living room."

That's integrity—and when it's genuine, it's the foundation of an attitude that will make other people want to make conversation with you.

16

High-Tech Talking

My dad worked for an aerospace company back in the 1960s. The company held an annual open house; here was a chance for our family to see where my dad spent most of his weekdays. It was a pretty high-tech (at the time) operation, and we were given guided tours of the facility. My strongest memory is when they showed us "the computer." It filled an entire room and displayed an array of flashing lights and whirling tapes. I remember being amazed when told what it could do.

At the time, the computer was state of the art. Workers used long, rectangular computer punch cards to input data into the computer. It was obvious to everyone that the future had arrived.

Around the same time, an office building was constructed near downtown Phoenix that was supposed to represent the most modern technology available. The building is shaped like a curved computer punch card, and the windows are positioned to look like the parts of the card that have been punched out. Today the building still stands as an unintentional monument to obsolescence.

In the early twenty-first century, email, social media, cell phones, and Internet communication have become the norm for many people. Carrying a smartphone or tablet enables people to communicate silently in the middle of a meeting without disturbing anyone around them. It seems efficient, since a person can begin and end a conversation with someone without ever leaving a meeting or event. But efficiency is different than effectiveness.

Technology in communication is part of our worldwide culture now, and we need to learn how to effectively balance electronic and live conversations. For example, it seems efficient when people use handheld devices to respond to emails and get them off their "to-do" list. But many of those emails might not be that important. Even though we're able to respond quickly, doing so might be taking us away from more important tasks and conversations. We focus on doing things right instead of doing the right things, putting activity ahead of results. Efficiency is "doing things right"; effectiveness is "doing the right things."

Smartphones and other portable electronics have made it much easier to connect with people quickly. Voice mail allows us to leave messages if the person isn't available, and texting puts people in touch instantly. In fact, by the time you're reading this, the current electronic tools will probably be obsolete. The list of advantages is long, and we wonder what we ever did without these tools. But that convenience doesn't mean our communication is better.

We've all had the experience of talking with someone on the phone and forming a visual impression of them. Then when we meet them in person, they look totally different than they sounded. On the phone, people can't see our facial expressions or body language. So it can be hard to get a clear picture of how the other person is responding. In this book we're trying to make conversation easier, not harder. Not having those visual clues available can really make the process tougher than it needs to be.

As we look at high-tech communication, the basic principles of making conversation still apply. We still have to deal with apprehension, approach people, and follow the rules of politeness and etiquette. Technology presents some unique challenges in those areas, and there are things to watch out for or do differently. No matter how we do it, the goal is the same: to communicate, connect, and converse with another person.

Whole courses have been written on how to handle voice mail, email, and other forms of communication technology. I won't try to cover every possible scenario. Instead, I'll simply reinforce the basics of making conversation and apply those specifics to contemporary connections.

Technological communication covers a number of areas, such as email, social media, forums and chat rooms, news groups, cell phones, instant messaging, and so on. We'll focus on the two main ones: written (email and other electronic communication) and verbal (phones and voice mail). Since chat rooms are common for many people, we'll spend a brief time applying our principles in that setting as well.

Effective Written Techniques

When electronic mail (email) first started, it was slow to catch on. Most people believed it was too informal and would never replace postal mail. It took time to compose a letter, address and stamp the envelope, and take it to a mailbox. But that was part of the attraction: the time it took demonstrated as much regard for the recipient as the letter itself.

But the fast pace of society has gradually caused email to be accepted, even preferred in many situations. The quantum leap in speed has become a positive rather than a negative for many people and organizations.

There are many advantages of electronic mail:

- It's a simple way to stay in touch with more people, in less time, more often.

- Email can be written and read at any hour of the day, since time zones are not an issue.

- The delivery is almost immediate, anywhere in the world.

- You save the cost of postage.

- The reader doesn't have to take notes on what you've said, since it's all in writing. Unlike a paper document, the recipient can copy and paste any section to forward or use in another document.

- Some people express themselves better in writing, so it's a good way to accurately express thoughts and feelings. That's also true with regular postal mail, but email combines the precision of writing with the convenience of speed and frequency.

- You can often reach people directly whom you wouldn't normally have access to, such as the CEO of an organization.

For many people, these advantages outweigh the disadvantages. Email has become not only an accepted form of communication but an expected one as well.

That doesn't minimize the disadvantages:

- You can't see the other person's body language or facial expressions, which make up 93 percent of how they communicate.
- It's easy to misread someone's meaning based solely on their choice of words.
- Since it's efficient, there could be a tendency to rely on this form of communication and avoid having live conversations. For a shy person, it can make the situation worse. The better they become online, the less incentive they have to force themselves out to practice in person.
- In writing, people can pretend to be something they're not, because you're not there to see their visual cues. The potential frequency of email can reinforce that inaccurate image.
- For kids, the stimulation of email and text messaging can be more exciting than reading books that help their imagination expand.
- Whatever you write casually is permanent and can be distributed widely.

These disadvantages can be particularly troublesome for quiet communicators, because they eliminate the nonverbal cues that make it easier to read people's reactions during a conversation. The key is balancing the use of email with other forms of connection.

Tips for Technical Talking

The same basic courtesies apply to email and other written electronic connections as any other type of communication:

- Make your emails concise. That doesn't necessarily mean short, but don't waste any extra words making your point.

- Follow the Golden Rule. Don't do or say anything online that you would avoid if you were speaking with someone face-to-face.

- Check and edit your emails as carefully as you do written documents. Remember that you're giving an impression through your words alone, without facial expressions or body language. Once you've hit "send," you don't get a chance to do it over. In a business context, people form an impression of your company based solely on their interaction with you. So don't get sloppy. Treat each email the way you would a letter or other document. Use paragraphs, complete sentences, active voice, and anything else you might use in another context.

- Most people are inundated with emails, so make their lives as simple as possible. Tell others exactly what you need in the subject line or the first sentence so they don't have to dig for the information.

- Learn the details of what your email program will do. Neglecting to do so is like buying a new camera but never reading the directions. The more you know, the more effective it will be. If you need help, you don't need to spend a lot of money to hire an advanced programmer. Just call your local college and find out who their best computer student is. They're probably working for a fast-food restaurant for minimum wage, so hire them for twice that amount. You get their expertise while they get a good income.

How to Avoid Electronic Pain

For all of its benefits, communicating electronically has some potentially painful outcomes that can be easily avoided with these reminders:

- Always check one last time that you're sending the right message to the right person. It's painful to have to do damage control after the fact.

- Be careful using abbreviations. They're commonly used in emails, but you could run into problems if the recipient doesn't understand. Abbreviations like LOL (laughing out loud), BTW (by the way) or EOM (end of message) only make sense when you know them. A colleague received a business email that ended with LOL. It was intended to show that the last sentence was humorous, but he thought it meant "lots of love." It took some explanation to reassure him of the meaning of the message.

- Be careful not to hit "reply all" when you only want to reply to the individual who wrote the email. You might find your personal discussion in the hands of dozens of other people.

- Don't forward jokes and stories unless you're sure the person wants to receive them. If they agree, don't forward those that have already been forwarded multiple times. Copy and paste the content, and add your own comments.

- Don't give lengthy emails about your opinions without the recipient's permission. You might be imposing when they would rather not spend time on that topic. I once had a lawyer charge me to write up some legal documents, and then he started sending me emails with his political view each month. Even though I agreed with his views, I thought it was inappropriate for him to assume I would want to read them. (He was charging me for his time; maybe I should have charged him for mine!)

- For special events, avoid using email notes and cards. An event like a wedding deserves a mailed card in most cases, and thank-you notes should be handwritten to make an impact. It might seem like no one is sending notes anymore since email is so common. But that's the exact reason to do it. You'll stand out in your communication with the other person when they're inundated with emails. A card or letter implies that it took time to write it, which demonstrate caring.

- Don't ignore emails someone has sent specifically to you. It's the same as if someone asked you a question in person and you turned and walked away. I once wrote a note of encouragement to a speaker I had respected for years. My note included a simple request, but I never heard back from him. His failure to respond probably was for a legitimate reason, but my opinion of him did not stay at the same level it had been before.

- Keep business emails business, and keep personal emails personal in the early stages of a relationship. Don't cross the line by making a business email "chatty" if you haven't developed a friendship that warrants it. Different people prefer different approaches, whether formal or informal. That's the message of this book: understand people's personality as a basis for knowing how to communicate with them.

- When sending an email to a group, make sure you learn how to hide their email addresses. I know the email addresses of several celebrities because someone who knew both of us simply inserted our names and email addresses in the address line. Any recipient on the list can see all of the other recipients and their addresses, which could feel like a breach of trust with some individuals.

- Avoid most types of humor in emails. Humor involves tone of voice, timing, and facial expressions to be effective. Those are missing in an email, so the chances of it succeeding are almost nonexistent.

- Don't let your Internet communication take the place of "in-person" conversations.

- Most people check their email and handle it without having to schedule time to do it. Spending too much time with it, however, can make you feel as if you don't have time for exercise, reading, or volunteer work. Don't let your life become one-dimensional because you feel shackled to your computer or smartphone.

Effective Social Media Techniques

The percentage of people using social media is huge. People who used to email now prefer texting, tweeting, or other instant communication where they don't have to wait for someone to check their email before responding. If the person has a phone, they can receive the message immediately.

Using social media like Facebook is like attending a social event. There are a lot of people you've never met and a few you might know well. Everyone has some common ground that brought them together. There are rules of etiquette that apply, and the same principles we've discussed about making conversation apply to this online forum. The primary difference is that since it's all done in writing, it doesn't matter what you look like and can be done in your pajamas.

If you think of social media in the same way you anticipate a social event or party, you'll have the approach that suits the occasion. You wouldn't enter a room and start talking about yourself, and you would make observations about the people in the room before deciding where to start connecting. For example, when commenting on a blog post, you don't want to barge in and start giving your opinions. "Listen" to the conversation as you enter to see what people are talking about. Then enter the discussion and make related comments. The advantage is that you have time to think through your response and can delete or reword something before sending it. Wouldn't it be great if we had the ability to edit our speech and delete things that didn't come out right in a live conversation?

In a chat room or forum, don't forget that you're communicating with real people in real time, just as you would in person. Treat people with courtesy, respect, and humor. Just because they can't see you doesn't mean you should come across any differently in writing than you would face-to-face. Affirm people in what they say and demonstrate that you're listening carefully by exploring their input in the conversation. Take turns in the conversation, allowing the normal flow of words without talking too much.

When you're ready to leave a chat room, don't just disappear. Exit in the same way you would in a live conversation: thank them for the conversation, briefly express your enjoyment of the time you've spent together and how much you're looking forward to your next conversation, and say good-bye. You want people to remember you in a positive way, so exit with meaning.

Effective Phone Techniques

People have been talking on the phone for years. So we can assume we all know the best way to use it effectively, right? Unfortunately, most of us have developed a few habits that interfere with getting the best results.

Let's start with a basic reminder of the purpose of using the phone: to connect with other people. We're having a conversation with someone just as we would in person. The only difference is that we can't see their facial expressions or body language. That's why our words and tone of voice become even more important.

Use the Golden Rule with people on the phone: interact with them the same way you'd like others to interact with you. Put yourself in their position: What is happening in the conversations that you respond to the most?

Often we might be hesitant to call someone because we're afraid of interrupting them and imposing. Instead of making that assumption, begin every phone conversation by asking them if this is a good time to talk or if you could schedule a time to talk later. This shows respect for them and lets you relax during the conversation. I often send an email ahead of time asking to schedule a phone appointment. Then I don't have to worry about inconveniencing others.

It's important to be as considerate on the phone as we would be in person. One way would be to update your voice mail greeting daily, making it clear to the person calling that you're interested in hearing from them. I have one friend whose voice mail says, "This is Mark. Today is July 19. I'll be unavailable until 3:00 and will check my voice mail later this afternoon and return calls by tomorrow at lunchtime." When I hear that greeting, I don't worry about whether he got my message when he doesn't call back right away. It's considerate and respectful of my time.

Since people can't see your gestures or facial expression on the phone, you have to make up for it with your tone of voice. Occasional verbal cues such as "Oh," "Uh-huh," "Really!" "That's interesting . . ." or "Tell me more" give people the signals that you're listening. When all they hear is silence as they're talking, it's like talking face-to-face with someone who simply responds with a blank stare.

Try this experiment: Engage a friend in a conversation while you're both standing up. But turn away from each other so you can't see any gestures or facial expressions. Notice the uncomfortable dynamics and what you have to do to connect effectively. That's exactly what it's like when you're on the phone, so it's a good way to become aware of what's happening in that interaction.

Using a person's name as you talk on the phone provides warmth in the conversation. Using it a bit more frequently than you would in person is like a verbal smile or handshake that helps you connect with the other person. But if you use the person's name too often, it will come across as insincere.

Don't be afraid of voice mail, but don't hide behind it either. It's a great tool for leaving a lengthy message with a chatty person. But don't make it the only way you connect. Before leaving a voice mail, craft it carefully. Succinctly outline the points you're going to make, give the details, and leave your phone number (twice, and slowly). I had an employer who used to delete my voice mails without finishing them if I got too wordy, because she didn't have time to waste while I rambled.

Because of that I've learned to plan my phone calls ahead of time. I jot down exactly what I want to cover (in order), what questions I have, and what action I need. I don't write it word-for-word so I'm not tempted to read my notes aloud.

If I'm calling someone in another city, I've found it valuable to do an internet search just before the call to find out what's happening in their area. If I know what the current temperature is in their area or the top story in their local news, it gives me some common ground to talk about during the call.

Be sure to treat receptionists, call-center personnel, and service personnel as real people, because that's what they are. If you treat them as an unavoidable delay, they'll respond in the same way. If you respect them, you can have a genuine connection with a person who normally doesn't expect it in their position. Find out the name of the person who answers the phone and remember it by writing it down.

Why? Because they *are* a real person, and it's the right thing to do. The fringe benefit is that if they feel good about you, they'll use their influence with the person you really want to talk to. But keep it genuine. Recognize how tough their job can be.

Tech Tips

Earlier, we discovered that only 7 percent of our communication comes through our words; the rest comes through the tone of our words and our body language. When we're talking by phone, we don't have the advantage of body language, which makes the tone of voice and word selection more important. In email and chat rooms, all we have is that 7 percent. That's why we need to balance electronic communication with face-to-face contacts. It may be more comfortable for some people, but it's basing an entire relationship on 7 percent of the potential communication. Without that other 93 percent, it's almost impossible to accurately know the other person well.

Because electronic communication is fairly simple, it's easy to get stuck with that one avenue of conversation. It will take different forms as technology changes over time. But remember to have live conversations as well so you don't become myopic. *Relationships* are what are important. Technology is simply a tool to enhance relationships—not the other way around.

17

A Mini-Course for Communication

I walked from Los Angeles to Denver last year.

It was a one thousand-mile journey. That might sound impressive, especially since I worked a full-time job and didn't take any time off work. But it wasn't as impossible as it might sound. For years I've talked about making that journey as an illustration in seminars, describing how the cumulative effect of taking little steps can give you huge results. If I walked three miles a day I knew I would cover one thousand miles in a year's time. After using the example so many times, I thought I should actually try it. So on January 1, I began my journey.

At the beginning of the year I calculated how many miles I should have covered on each date of the year to keep me on track. Then I found an online pedometer where I could click my beginning point and add my mileage each day along a map of the country. So I "started" at the ocean at the Santa Monica pier and began following the route of Interstate 10. Most days I would go to the river trail near our house and cover the three miles. Some days I would break the walking up between morning, lunchtime, and evening. Sometimes I would walk more, while I might skip entire days occasionally.

It took some commitment to fit that walking into my schedule, but I was amazed at the distance I began to cover. It was only a few weeks before I had left metropolitan Los Angeles behind and was walking through the desert towns of Boron and Barstow. I picked up my pace in Las Vegas and strolled through southern Utah. Most days I would check the temperature of the city closest to where I was walking to get a sense of what conditions were on that day.

On December 31, I clicked the online map to find myself entering the Denver city limits.

You can look at learning to make conversation in the same way. Getting from where we are now to a place of conversational confidence might seem like a huge task. But if we break it into small steps and measure our progress, we'll be amazed at how much "ground" we can cover over time. Small steps taken consistently yield big results.

Learning to converse confidently may seem as if it involves a steep learning curve. But if we plan carefully and take the process step-by-step, using persistence and patience, we'll achieve our goal. The measurement part is important, because otherwise we'll just be looking at how much distance remains to reach our goal. But it's important to see how far we've come.

Where Do We Start?

The best place to start is to realize that you don't have to become something you're not. Instead, you want to:

- Recognize your temperament and personality.
- Accept the uniqueness of that personality.
- Develop it, using it as the basis for how you interact with others.

It's a matter of working from our strengths. Learning to make conversation will become a realistic goal when we follow a carefully designed process using sequential steps: examination, partnership, preparation, observation, progression, evaluation, and celebration.

Step One: Examination

When my father-in-law built a cabin in the mountains, he didn't just grab some lumber and start construction. Since he was going to build on a heavily forested slope, the cabin would have tumbled down the mountain if he hadn't done a thorough site evaluation first. He hired professionals to check the soil compaction, drainage, and conditions of the land. The professionals' input combined with a blueprint that reflected the type of cabin he wanted to build set the project up for success.

The same is true in making conversation. It's easy to want to jump in and start trying, but it's important to have a clear picture of the terrain. It's an important step but one that's easy to bypass. If you don't think through your resources and study the conversational terrain, you might end up feeling frustrated with your results.

Do a careful study of your temperament—your unique gifts and abilities that make you who you are. Think through the results of the test you took in chapter 3 and see what tools you have to work with.

Then evaluate the picture you have of what you want to accomplish against the reality of your personality. If you're an introvert but said you wanted to be the life of the party that everyone gravitates to, you might want to rethink your goal. Your goal needs to be realistic in light of your uniqueness. When you get that type of congruence, there's a great chance for success. When you capitalize on how God made you, you have the best chance at being effective making conversation your way, not someone else's way.

Next, spend time analyzing what you tell yourself. In chapter 15 we talked about attitude and self-talk. Separate what is true from what is an inaccurate perception. If you recognize the parts of your self-talk that are not true, you can rewrite those perspectives and base them on reality. Analyze the filters that have made you who you are (chapter 4). What are the dynamics that shape the way you think? It's a great way to analyze your self-talk.

Step Two: Partnership

An introvert friend and I were discussing how many tools we have in our garages. It seems that when something needs to be done, we don't want to impose on someone else for help. So instead of borrowing tools, we buy what we need for the job and do it ourselves.

That might work for home repairs, but it's hard to stay committed to an area in which we want to grow if we don't have someone to hold us accountable. We feel energetic about our new endeavor, but there's no one to lift us up when we're discouraged. That's why there is so much value in going on this journey with a partner.

Find another person who is about at your level of conversational skill to commit to making progress with you. Read this book together and then chart out a plan to help you improve. The activities you choose should be concrete and specific. Instead of saying, "We'll try to be more outgoing this week," decide "We'll initiate a thirty-second conversation with three new people this week." Plan for a time to check each other's progress, provide encouragement, and help each other get a realistic view of your successes and challenges.

A few years ago my son and a good friend decided to work together to improve their conversational skills with the opposite sex. They talked about new ways to initiate conversations and made a chart to keep track of how many times they made a contact during each week. My son's friend had an advantage, since he was a pilot for a small commercial airline. While making the flight announcements he would say, "... and if any single women are interested in having coffee with a single pilot, just drop your name and number with the pilot standing in the cockpit door as you exit the plane."

Step Three: Preparation

When explorers go into unknown territory, their survival depends on preparation. Since they don't know what they're going to encounter, they make sure they study the terrain, get their tools in order, and anticipate any situation that could happen. The more prepared they are, the more confident they'll be in new situations.

Think through an upcoming conversation and consider how

you could approach the other person with a genuine attitude of caring. It will probably come from thinking about them realistically, considering what their view of life might be. Consider their value as a person, as well as their struggles, real-life concerns, and fears. See them as a human being, not as a project.

Prepare a list of generic questions you might ask in any conversation. When you're meeting a specific person, customize those questions to that unique encounter before you make the connection. Write them out and review them before the meeting takes place.

Think of how you'll answer someone the next time they ask, "How are you?" Instead of responding, "Fine," think of a single sentence that hints at something going on in your life that would be a safe conversational opener. Don't press the subject; just wait and see if they take the bait.

It's also good to prepare a list of topics you know something about and could discuss if necessary. This can give you confidence in those potential conversational lulls that happen to everyone.

Step Four: Observation

Every time you have an opportunity, observe other people carefully. Listen to their words and look carefully at their facial expressions and body language. Be aware of what they do, what they say, and how they manage their side of a conversation. As you compare their conversational style with yours, you can determine if some of the approaches they use might be effective for you. Watch how they handle tough conversations and contrast their approach with the one you might expect to use.

This is especially helpful during a conversation when you're feeling fearful. Try to notice the things that most people ignore: eye color, how many times they blink as they speak, or any facial gestures that might go unnoticed to a casual observer. Consciously focusing on them instead of yourself keeps you so busy in the moment that you'll no longer have feelings of anxiety.

Observing yourself is another way of getting accurate information about how you come across to others. Set up a tape recorder near your phone and turn it on for your next few phone calls, recording only your side of the conversation. Listen to it later so you can hear how you come across to others. Don't be too hard on yourself; most people don't like the sound of their own voice. You hear your voice differently inside your head because of the resonance of the bone structures. But you'll be able to detect speech patterns, tone of voice, and phrases you didn't know you were using.

Step Five: Progression

After you've taken the time to evaluate the situation, find a partner, make careful preparation, and observe others, it's time to practice the conversational journey. With your tools in hand, you can feel confident as you begin. Consider these suggestions to move effectively through the process:

- Make a list of the behaviors you want to implement. Take them one at a time and practice each one until you've gained some confidence before moving to the next one.

- Start small if you need to. Begin by smiling at ten people in the mall. The next day, smile and say "Hi." The next day, smile, say "Hi," and ask them if they could give you the correct time. If you keep your initial steps nonthreatening and simple, you'll build your confidence.

- Pick five people you want to meet. Plan carefully how you'll approach each one and go through the process with them. Take notes after each conversation to remind you of the topics you covered, as well as new areas to explore the next time you meet. It might feel like you're treating them like a project instead of a person. But you're simply focusing your efforts to care about them.

- Make sure to appear open to conversation with others. Take off your headphones at the gym and avoid hiding behind a book in a public setting. Those types of things are like wearing a sign that says "No Trespassing."

- If someone initiates a conversation with you, take advantage of it. Realize that they just saved you from the challenge of initiating a conversation, so the tough part is done. You're free to explore the conversation and practice your skills in a safe environment.

- Join a group where you have something in common with others and will be working side-by-side with them. Volunteer work with a local church or charitable organization provides a laboratory for connecting where the common ground is already established.

- Use the people you know to connect with people you don't know. Spend time with your friends in social situations and you'll have a way of meeting their contacts in a friendly setting.

- At any social event, make it a point to meet three people you don't know, remember their names, and use their names at the end of the event as you say good-bye.

- If you've had a good conversation, get the person's email or mailing address. Send them a note a few days later expressing your appreciation for their time, refer to something you talked about, and even attach an article they might find interesting. This is a great way to keep yourself fresh in their minds for future connections.

- Take your time. You've spent a lifetime with your current conversational habits, so be patient as you pace yourself through the journey.

Step 6: Evaluation and Celebration

Don't minimize the impact of this step. It's common to exaggerate our failures and minimize our successes. But that approach can be damaging to our self-talk as we're making progress. Be realistic about the things that go wrong. Realize that a single shaky conversation doesn't define your efforts; it's just one more step you've gotten out of the way toward success.

This is one area where it's valuable to have a partner in the process. As you celebrate each other's victories and give perspective about the mistakes, you have an incentive to continue on your journey.

Talking with Your Eyes Wide Open

It's been said that the best defense is a good offense. That's why it's valuable to be aware of things we do that could actually lead to painful conversations (so we can avoid them), as well as things that make conversations work well (so we can do them).

Things to Avoid

- Don't ignore someone else's feelings. We might assume that if we don't acknowledge someone's feelings or if we minimize them, those feelings will simply disappear. In reality, this makes the situation worse. Use listening skills to identify with what the other person is feeling and offer support. When done genuinely, this builds trust with others.

- When someone is upset, don't try to fix them. Strong emotion needs to be felt, not swept under the rug. Most of us have been in relationships in which we shared the deep concerns of our heart, but the other person tried to fix our feelings or solve the problem. It feels as if they're more interested in giving advice than in listening to our heart.

  In *The View from a Hearse*, Joe Bayly described the grief surrounding the death of three of his sons at different times. Sitting in the hospital with one son on his deathbed, Bayly described the comments from visitors who didn't know what to say. He knew they meant well, but he just wanted them to leave so he could handle his grief alone.

  Finally a friend walked in without a word and sat down next to him. He didn't talk or ask leading questions. He just simply sat beside him. Occasionally Bayly would make a comment and his friend would respond briefly. He didn't pry or try to come up with answers. He just identified with what Joe was feeling. When the friend got up to leave, Joe hated to see him go, since he was providing exactly what he needed without trying to make it "all better." When you're about to lose one of your kids, it's just not going to get better. At that point you simply need people to come alongside and walk through the journey with you.

As Bayly wrote, "Don't try to 'prove' anything to a survivor. An arm about the shoulder, a firm grip of the hand, a kiss: these are the proofs grief needs, not logical reasoning."[14]

- Don't let your mind wander when it takes someone a long time to "get to the point." Recognize that it's happening and concentrate on what is being said. Make sure you don't jump ahead, filling in the blanks when they have too many pauses. They'll feel rushed and think you're anxious to get out of the conversation.

- Don't assume that your initial impression of a person is accurate. The longer we talk with someone, the more we learn what's under the surface. We should assume that no matter whom we're talking to, what we're hearing and seeing isn't the whole story.

I recently taught a seminar for a major utility. The first person who entered the room engaged me in conversation, telling me about his job, how he thought people should perform differently, and how much experience he had with the company. My first impression was that he was arrogant and a monopolizer, not someone I was looking forward to having in class for the next three days. Those types of people typically tend to throw group dynamics into a tailspin.

But as the day progressed, I found out that he was in charge of safety for the entire utility company and that someone had just died the night before because they violated safety procedures. What I interpreted as arrogance was simply his passion for safety coming through his conversation. By the end of the three days, he had won the hearts of the entire class with his sensitive passion for the lives of the company's employees.

- When you tell stories about your life, make sure they're accurate. You never know when someone you're talking with was at the same event and knows that you're embellishing the details. From that point on, they'll question your integrity.

- Don't let a conversation get into a debate when you've just met someone. If they don't know you, they haven't developed trust in you. Without that trust, they don't have a reason to invest the time in you or your views.

- Avoid these conversation killers:

  Giving unsolicited advice (it comes across as arrogance)

  Correcting people (their story details, their grammar, or their conclusions)

  Not showing interest (so why bother talking?)

  Gossip (they assume you'll be talking about them with the next person)

  Finishing people's sentences for them (that's their job, not yours)

Things to Do

- Listen carefully to what the other person is saying and feeling before presenting your position. Our tendency is to immediately rush in with our perspective, telling them how they should feel or what they should do. But when we reply before deeply listening to them, our ideas might not even be heard. If we give unwanted advice when we haven't listened, we're implying that they can't handle the situation on their own.

- Make it your goal in each conversation to discover something you didn't already know about the other person, no matter how long you've been friends.

  Dick has been a good friend for over a decade. When he and his wife were sitting on our patio last week, we were watching the birds swarming a bird feeder hanging from our eaves. He began describing each bird by name and characteristics and talked about his years of self-taught knowledge about birds. For as long as I had known him, I never knew about that expertise.

  Almost everyone has knowledge or experience we don't know about. Make it a point to find out as you explore each conversation.

- Use the Golden Rule: "Do unto others as you would have them do unto you." Think about the things people do in a conversation that you find rewarding and practice those same things with them.

- At the beginning of a conversation, assume that you've been asked to repeat what you've heard to your spouse or friend at a later time. You'll listen better and retain more information, since you'll be responsible for re-creating the discussion points accurately.

- Decide that you genuinely want to listen. You can't fake it. Somehow, that disinterest will come through your body language or facial expressions.

  I've learned that taking a moment just before a conversation to remind myself to listen carefully makes a big difference in my focus. I have to decide that it's important and that I genuinely want to understand.

- As you're listening, remember the presence of the conversational filters discussed in chapter 4. What the other person is saying is being filtered through their life experience and perspectives. So while you think you understand, recognize that there might be a different or deeper meaning than you initially thought.

Wrapping It Up

Your job is to handle your side of the conversation, practicing and perfecting your technique and approach. You're not responsible for how the other person responds, so don't let it define your perspective. You won't connect perfectly with everyone, because no one is perfect.

It's kind of like shopping for produce. When you enter a grocery store, you head for the fruits and vegetables. They're probably all good for you, but some attract you more than others. You'll look at them all but end up selecting which ones you want to take home. Just because you don't buy them all doesn't mean you're a poor shopper. You're simply choosing which ones will meet your own needs.

We're not "shopping" for conversational partners. But as we engage a variety of people in conversations, we'll choose which ones we want to continue connecting with while enjoying our brief time with others.

Be realistic. Start slow, monitor your progress, and enjoy the ride. Work in your comfort zone but gradually push the boundaries. Over time, your comfort zone will grow.

You can be comfortable and confident in conversations, but you don't want to totally eliminate the creative tension that makes for a good interaction. There's no such thing as a casual conversation. Anything worthwhile takes effort, but you'll be operating from a position of confidence.

18

Meeting Face-to-Face

I don't play much golf, which could explain why I'm not very good at it. It always amazes me to watch someone who's really good—how they can put the ball almost exactly where they want it to go. I once watched a pro golfer hit the ball past the green on a slope; it rolled back to within inches of the cup. And he did it on purpose.

That's why people enjoy watching the Olympics. You get to see world-class athletes do things that boggle the mind.

There is one important thing to remember as we watch these gifted athletes: *They weren't always that good.* Maybe they had natural talent, but they started slowly and practiced over and over. They reached elite levels because they did what they were gifted to do and practiced to hone their skills.

Not everyone will become a "world-class conversationalist." But that's OK. Just because you can't play golf like Tiger Woods doesn't mean you can't play well and enjoy the game.

In the same way, anyone can practice the skills of conversation to become confident in any situation.

Fortunately, success in making conversation is possible when we start small, practice, and grow. We don't have to be perfect; we have to be effective.

Rick Warren suggests that everyone has a purpose that involves impacting the lives of others. When our conversational skills help us build relationships, we have the opportunity to impact our world. That's why Mother Teresa said her mission was "to be a pencil in the hand of God."

In a world of fast-paced electronic communication, there is an even greater need for the dynamics of face-to-face interaction. Technology can be a great tool for communication, but it shouldn't replace live conversations. People's lives are changed through heart-to-heart conversation, not efficient emails.

Spend time developing your conversational skills and you'll see steady improvement. That, in turn, will help you achieve all the things you want to accomplish in life. God wants us to touch the lives of others; making conversation is the basis of making it happen.

It's great to learn cooking, gardening, or car repair. But learning to make conversation is the one skill that is foundational for everything else you do. It's like the engine in your car. You could have the most expensive car in the world, but if it has a tiny engine, it won't do what it was designed to do.

Four Keys to Conversational Success

We've covered a lot of ground in this book. But we could summarize four crucial steps:

1. Function uniquely.
2. Prepare thoroughly.
3. Explore expectantly.
4. Focus outwardly.

Function Uniquely

My wife and I visited a small art gallery by the beach a few years ago. We saw one picture that looked like a checkerboard made up of pastel construction paper cut into squares. It was mounted on a canvas and suspended in a glass case. It was interesting and seemed well-done. But then my eyes caught the price tag: $250,000. Not being art connoisseurs, we asked the manager what it was about a piece of art that could possibly make it worth a quarter of a million dollars. He simply pointed to the signature at the bottom. It wasn't a name we recognized, but he assured us that anyone in the art community would recognize the name in an instant.

The value came from the creator. People are willing to pay more for an original than they are for a copy of the same piece. It's that uniqueness that sets it apart from everything else.

We humans almost always seem dissatisfied with who we are. If we have straight hair, we wish it were curly. If we have curly hair, we pay to have it straightened. We're always too something or not enough something else.

It's common for introverts to want to be like extroverts, because it looks like extroverts have an easier time handling life and relationships. There is value in seeing how they communicate, because we can study those patterns and adopt the appropriate ones for our own use. It may also be common for extroverts to dominate a conversation, but there's much to be learned and gained from listening. Either way, if we persist in trying to become something other than the person we were born to be, we rob ourselves—and the world—of the most valuable asset we have: our uniqueness. That's the one thing that will make us more effective in making conversation than anything else. When we accept our personality and develop it rather than trying to change it, we have the potential for making dynamic conversation.

We don't have to be a certain way just because someone else is. We have to be *us*.

Prepare Thoroughly

Teaching a seminar in a city or hotel that is unfamiliar used to be stressful for me. Finding my way through traffic while trying to follow a map to an obscure location took its toll on my emotional energy. I've learned a better approach.

I arrive in town the day before the seminar, and later that evening I'll drive to the seminar location to scout out the territory without having to fight traffic. I'll choose the best route and find out exactly where to park. If it's a hotel, I'll go inside and locate the meeting room where I'll be setting up. It only takes a short time to do this "discovery" process but makes a world of difference in how I feel the next morning. Careful preparation reduces my stress level.

In the same way, the time spent getting ready for a conversation can make the difference in the success of the encounter. The more you think it through ahead of time, the more confident you'll feel.

Preparation isn't accidental, and it's worth the effort. It

might take a while to make it a habit, but consistent practice will make it more natural.

Preparing for a conversation is like pushing a car. The hardest part is getting started. Once you're "on a roll," you're OK. So think through your options for getting the conversation rolling. Over time it will become an automatic part of the process.

No matter what your conversational skill level is, there's always room for improvement. Preparation is one of the simplest ways to make conversation more effective.

Explore Expectantly

There are two concepts in this step: *explore* and *expectantly*. *Exploring* is the basis of everything this book has been discussing: finding out what tools you have, learning how to use them, implementing them to find common ground with others, and then exploring new conversational territory. *Expectantly* means looking forward to an exciting journey. When you're in the early stages of learning these skills, it might be hard to imagine the process being exciting. But like mastering a sport, the process becomes fun when your competence grows. Success won't happen overnight. It's a skill set that takes time to master, but it can be done easily by moving through small steps consistently.

Be careful not to have a mind-set that sees the process as harder than it actually is. Like any worthwhile skill that you don't know, it seems hard when you're at the bottom of the learning curve. But if you learn to explore gradually and practice your new skills, you'll be able to talk to anyone, anywhere. You won't have to be intimidated by those conversations because, like any other skill, you've learned what to do when it occurs.

During any learning process, it's good to keep track of your progress. Doing it in writing solidifies that process and gives you a measurable way to see your progress realistically. You'll be able to focus on how far you've come instead of how far you need to go. When that happens, you'll gain confidence.

Focus Outwardly

Zig Ziglar says that if you help everyone you meet get what they need, you'll get what you need in the process. That's why you want to focus on others instead of yourself. If you focus on your performance, you'll never feel the fulfillment that comes from healthy relationships. But if you learn to focus on the other person, personal fulfillment will be a fringe benefit.

When you're in a social situation and you're wondering whether you should approach a certain person to initiate a conversation, listen carefully to your self-talk. You'll probably find that you're evaluating what the other person will be thinking if you approach them. If you feel they'll have a negative opinion of you when you walk up to them, ask yourself what is causing that assumption. Is it something in their body language or facial expression? Or are you simply projecting your own fear onto them, anticipating a negative reaction?

Ask yourself, "What is the worst possible thing that could happen?" Then go for it. See how close the reality matches your assumption. In the majority of cases, you'll be pleasantly surprised. After the conversation, make sure you consciously compare how it turned out with how you expected it to turn out. You'll find that most people will respond positively when you approach them with genuine interest.

Keep your conversations positive, since that sets the tone for future conversations. If the other person enjoyed their time with you, they'll have a positive feeling when you meet again in the future. They'll remember how you made them feel the first time, and they'll look forward to feeling that way again. Relax and enjoy the process. Stay lighthearted; don't take yourself too seriously.

Be ready for chance encounters. You won't always be the one initiating every conversation; others will initiate with you. When they do, your preparation will be your strength. As soon as someone approaches you, anticipate the opportunity to practice what you've learned. You never know when these "accidental" connections can impact your entire future.

There's one more reason it's important to focus on others. As your conversational skills improve and you practice them with others, you're actually giving them a chance to improve their skills as well. They might not even recognize what's happening, but you've brought them into your workshop to practice your communication skills together.

A Final Word

No matter what your personality style, you can make conversing one of the most rewarding and positive things you can do in life. Since you really don't have a choice (we have to make conversation to make it through life), you have every motivation to take the steps to get really good at it. By consciously working on your skills, you'll be able to enjoy connections you already have and look forward to new conversations. You can build your skills at a safe, comfortable speed, using methods that fit your style and moving into new skill levels when you've mastered the current ones.

The phone company used to have a slogan that said, "Reach out and touch someone." Take that challenge. Be yourself, develop your skills within your own unique personality, and reach out to others. You'll find yourself on a lifelong journey that can change your life—and impact the lives of everyone you meet!

Notes

1. Burton Stevenson, *The Home Book of Quotations* (New York: Dodd, Mead & Co., 1967), 14.

2. Dale Carnegie, *How to Win Friends and Influence People* (New York: Pocket Books, 1981), 54.

3. Isabel Briggs Myers, *Gifts Differing: Understanding Personality Type* (Palo Alto, CA: Consulting Psychologists Press, 1980).

4. Roger Von Oech, *A Kick in the Seat of the Pants* (New York: Harper Paperbacks, 1986).

5. John Trent, *The Treasure Tree* (Nashville: Nelson, 1982).

6. Rick Warren, *The Purpose-Driven Life* (Grand Rapids: Zondervan, 2002), 17.

7. Larry King, *How to Talk to Anyone, Anytime, Anywhere* (New York: Random House, 1994), 40.

8. Albert Mehrabian, *Silent Messages: Implicit Communication of Emotions and Attitudes* (Belmont, CA: Wadsworth, 1980), 75.

9. Hans Selye, *Stress without Distress* (New York: NAL Penguin, 1974).

10. William Glasser, *Reality Therapy* (New York: Harper & Row, 1975).

11. Briggs Myers, *Gifts Differing*, 69–73.

12. Henry Drummond, *The Greatest Thing in the World* (New York: Revell, 1891), 30.

13. H. Dale Burke, *Less Is More Leadership* (Eugene, OR: Harvest House, 2004), 71.

14. Joseph Bayly, *The View from a Hearse* (Elgin, IL: Cook, 1969), 40.

Mike Bechtle has a unique blend of ministry and corporate experience—from eighteen years in churches and Christian universities to more than 2,500 time- and life-management seminars taught to many of the Fortune 500 companies. He is the author of *Evangelism for the Rest of Us,* and his articles have appeared in publications such as *Discipleship* Journal, *Moody, Eternity,* Pastors.com, and *Entrepreneur.* He has been speaking at churches and conventions since 1974. After receiving his master's degree at Talbot School of Theology, he received his doctorate in higher and adult education from Arizona State University. Currently a senior training consultant for FranklinCovey Company, he lives in Fullerton, California. For information about speaking engagements and seminars, visit

www.mikebechtle.com
www.confidentconversation.net

Meet Mike Bechtle at
WWW.MIKEBECHTLE.COM

- Read his blog
- Follow his speaking schedule
- Find recommended resources

and connect with him on 📘 **and** 🐦 **.**

YOU **DON'T** HAVE TO BE CONTROLLED BY **DIFFICULT PEOPLE!**

Communication expert Mike Bechtle shows you how to stop being a victim of other people's craziness. With common-sense wisdom and proactive advice that you can put into practice immediately, Bechtle gives you a proven strategy to handle crazy people—and stay sane while doing it.